D0084453

VARIATIONS

Reading Skills/Oral Communication for Beginning Students of ESL

Pat Duffy

New York University
American Language Institute

Illustrated by Daphne Fraser

PRENTICE HALL REGENTS
Englewood Cliffs, New Jersey 07632

Library of Congress Cataloging-in-Publication Data

Duffy, Pat, (date)
    Variations : reading skills-oral communication for
beginning students of ESL.

    1. English language—Text-books for foreign speakers.
I. Fraser, Daphne. II. Title.
PE1128.D824 1986   428.2′4   85–30025
ISBN 0–13–940503–8

Cover design: Lundgren Graphics, Ltd.
Manufacturing buyer: Harry Baisley

©1986 by Prentice Hall Regents
Prentice-Hall, Inc.
A Simon & Schuster Company
Englewood Cliffs, New Jersey 07632

Printed in the United States of America

20 19 18 17 16 15 14 13 12

ISBN   0-13-940503-8

Prentice-Hall International (UK) Limited, *London*
Prentice-Hall of Australia Pty. Limited, *Sydney*
Prentice-Hall Canada Inc., *Toronto*
Prentice-Hall Hispanoamericana, S.A., *Mexico*
Prentice-Hall of India Private Limited, *New Delhi*
Prentice-Hall of Japan, Inc., *Tokyo*
Simon & Schuster Asia Pte. Ltd., *Singapore*
Editora Prentice-Hall do Brasil, Ltda., *Rio de Janeiro*

Contents

Preface

For the beginning student of English as a Second Language (ESL), a little reading can go a long way. Brief, entertaining readings are often the most productive for beginning students, since these tend to curb frustration by keeping interest and motivation high. The short passages contained in the fifteen chapters of *Variations* have been student-tested for high interest level. Both the readings and the sometimes unique exercises that follow them have proved to promote a high degree of verbal interaction among class members.

Variations introduces some fresh subject matter into ESL lessons and gets away from the old familiar topics. Passage topics range from public affection in different cultures and UFO experiences to international cuisine, superstitions, and the Amish people of the Pennsylvania Dutch country. The readings aim to expand the students' knowledge of the world as they expand their knowledge of the new language. Students will find the readings informative and often provocative.

Although *Variations* is not a grammar book, the major reading in each chapter has a structural focus to help cultivate and sharpen students' awareness of grammatical accuracy. Teachers can use the readings to introduce or reinforce a particular structure.

Illustrations accompanying each chapter help clarify the subject matter and define new vocabulary for each passage. The illustrations are also to be used for pre-reading exercises. The teacher may ask students to look at the pictures before they read the passages and elicit vocabulary and topic content from them. The pre-reading questions in each chapter also prepare students for the subject matter of the readings.

The reading passages are brief and compact so that students will be prompted to comment on or expand upon their content, thus stimulating class discussion. Also, because of their brevity, the readings do not drain the student of the energy needed to analyze them for structure, vocabulary, and meaning. The wide variety of exercises that follows each reading is designed to help students get the maximum advantage from their first experience reading in English.

All chapters include reading/listening exercises, since recent research indicates that these two activities are among the most beneficial for beginning students. Certainly, showing students the relationship between reading and listening is vital. Frank Smith points out the importance of this connection in his book *Understanding Reading,* in which he contends that "people learn to read by being read to." The teacher is therefore encouraged to read aloud to students the title passage in each chapter, while the students follow along silently. The teacher might want to stop after reading one or two sentences of the passage to ask one of the corresponding comprehension questions that follow the reading (sentences in passages and questions have corresponding numbers). In this way, a dialoguelike exchange is set up between teacher and student (or student and student).

Wilga Rivers has discussed the importance of what she calls an *interactive approach* in the language-learning process. Rivers maintains that a sense of *communicative exchange* is essential in promoting comprehension and fluency in a new language. The format of *Variations,* with its combination of comprehension questions and text, lends itself to such an approach.

In addition, students are taught to develop such basic reading skills as guessing meanings from context (and other vocabulary-building exercises) and identifying the main idea and supporting details. Some chapters include supplementary readings in which students are asked to skim for the main idea and scan for specific details.

Each of the major readings has a grammatical focus, and chapters therefore contain exercises that provide practice with a particular structure. Students are given further opportunity to practice new structures and vocabulary in the group activities section of each chapter. These activities allow students to practice the new material on their own, thus making the crucial transition from passive understanding to active usage.

There are also activities that utilize James Asher's total physical response (TPR) technique. These incorporate various games and exercises in which students are required to respond physically to action commands given by the teacher (or other students). Typical games include *Simon Says, Charades,* and exercises in which students direct one another in the making of holiday costumes, decorations, recipes, and other creations. Directions given make use of the vocabulary items in the chapters. Many of the exercises in *Variations* seek to transform words from sight to sound to action, so they become real for students and are no longer merely alien sounds that students must struggle to remember. Research shows that physical actions and cues can be a great aid to retaining new material, and my experience with students has found this to be so.

The diversity of exercises in *Variations* makes it appropriate for both academic and nonacademic programs of study. Teachers are free to choose from the exercises those that are suitable for their students.

The order of the chapters reflects their level of difficulty, and subsequent chapters often contain structural and vocabulary items from previous chapters. However, it is not absolutely necessary to follow the chapters in sequence. Teachers may choose the sequence most appropriate for their classes.

For too long there has been a dearth of readers for beginning students of ESL. *Variations* seeks to help remedy this situation. It is my hope that teachers as well as students will find the reading content to be of interest. Certainly, there is nothing like teacher interest to help generate student interest.

Acknowledgments

The influence and energy of many people made the completion of this book possible, and I want to thank some of those persons now.

First, I'd like to thank Allan Kent Dart, whose kind help and encouragement I cannot overestimate as a prime motivating force in the writing of this book. I thank him greatly.

A second big thank you goes to Maxine Steinhaus, whose friendship and feedback were invaluable in helping me see this project through from beginning to end. Another thank you to Carolyn Graham, with whom I had the very good fortune to share a class at New York University. The *irregular verb rhyme* in Chapter 3 was inspired by her wonderful jazz chants. Still another thank you to Yatsen Chan, with whom I've worked on several ESL projects, and who provided the inspiration for the "Practice with Ordinal Numbers" exercise in Chapter 14. Thanks also to Lorraine Lapetina for always expressing confidence in my project and for suggesting the role-play exercise in Chapter 2. Thank you to Ann Kennedy and George Spanos for their friendship and moral support. More thanks to Shelley Scammell for her forthright advice and to Jim Tamulis for his assistance with research for the film articles in Chapter 3. A deep thanks to Jimmy Young, whose great encouragement and love I can never forget.

Many thanks to the administrations of the American Language Institute, New York University, and the English Language Center, LaGuardia Community College, for providing an educational atmosphere conducive to creativity and experimentation, where I felt free and encouraged to test my materials. Of course, a big thank you to all my wonderful ESL students—my most valuable critics.

A special thanks to Josh Cohen just for being there, and at the right time.

Most of all, I'd like to thank my father, the late John Duffy, for all those inspiring years of "kitchen-table" discussions and debates that made me see that so many things were possible.

Pat Duffy

To my father and mother

chapter 1

What Is Everybody Doing Now?

The Present Continuous Tense

Pre-reading Questions

Look at the picture. What are the different people in the picture doing?
Are any of your classmates doing the same things?

What Is Everybody Doing Now?

Look around your class. Probably most of the students are paying attention to their studies.[1] Because they are thinking about their studies, they are probably not paying attention to their gestures, or body movements.[2] For example, as you look around your classroom, you are noticing, perhaps, that some students are scratching their heads while they are doing their work.[3] Other students are squeezing their chins. Others are crossing and uncrossing their legs. Still others are rubbing their eyes or pulling their ears.[4] Maybe a few students are opening their mouths and yawning.[5] A few others are covering their mouths with their hands.[6] Possibly several others are stretching their arms or their fingers.[7] Perhaps one or two students are even putting their pens or pencils between their teeth and chewing them![8] When people are not paying attention to their gestures, we can sometimes catch them doing funny things.[9]

1. What are most of the students probably doing?
2. What are most of the students probably not doing?
3. What are some students doing while they are working?
4. What are other students doing?
5. What are a few students doing?
6. What are a few others doing?
7. What are several others doing?
8. What are one or two students doing?
9. When can we sometimes catch people doing funny things?
10. Now, do the actions described in this reading, or point to a classmate who is doing them.

The Present Continuous Tense

We can use the present continuous tense to describe an action that is happening *now:*

subject	verb *to be*	verb + **-ing**	object
I	am	studying	English.
You (we, they)	are	studying	English.
He (she, it)	is	studying	English.

To form a question, we reverse the position of the subject and the verb *to be*:

verb *to be*	subject	verb + -ing	object
Am	I	studying	English?
Are	you (we, they)	studying	English?
Is	he (she, it)	studying	English?

To make a negative sentence, we put the word *not* after the verb *to be*:

subject	verb *to be*	*not*	verb + -ing	object
I	am	not	studying	English.
You (we, they)	are	not	studying	English.
He (she, it)	is	not	studying	English.

Often, we put *are* and *not* together, and *is* and *not* together to form the following contractions:

are + not = aren't   is + not = isn't

Vocabulary

Write the appropriate present continuous tense verbs in the spaces provided. Do not use the same word more than one time.

chew	open	scratch
cover	pay attention (to)	squeeze
cross/uncross	pull	stretch
look (around)	**put**	think (about)
notice	rub	yawn

Examples

a. I __am looking around__ the room to find my friend.

b. He __is crossing__ his legs to change his position.

c. They __are putting__ the flowers in the vase.

1. They _____ because they are tired.

2. She _____ her mouth to speak.

3. You _____ gum.

4. The cat _____ its nails on the tree.

5. They _____ their problems.

6. He _____ the door to open it.

7. We _____ the other students' gestures.

8. The child _____ his sore arm.

Now supply the appropriate noun:

arm(s)	gesture(s)	studies
chin(s)	body movements	pencil(s)
ear(s)	hand(s)	pen(s)
eye(s)	head(s)	tooth (teeth)
finger(s)	leg(s)	

Example

d. We use our _ears_ to hear.

9. We see with our _____.

10. She is pointing with her _____.

11. The _____ is below the mouth.

12. In class, students are usually paying attention to their

    _____.

13. We use our _____ to walk.

14. The students are raising their _____ to answer the teacher's

    question.

15. She is carrying the child in her _____.

Continue to fill in the appropriate noun for these other parts of the body:

ankle(s)	hair	nose(s)
cheek(s)	hip(s)	shoulder(s)
face(s)	knee(s)	stomach(s)
fingernail(s), nail(s)	mouth(s)	waist(s)
foot **(feet)**		

Example
e. He is putting his *feet* inside his shoes.

16. She is combing her _____.

17. He is wearing a belt around his _____.

18. Many women put red polish on their _____.

19. Children often have rosy _____.

20. The waist is just above the _____.

21. The _____ connects the leg to the foot.

22. The _____ is in the middle of the leg.

23. The _____ is in the middle of the face.

Now supply the appropriate adjective:

few   most of the (noun)   several   some

Example
f. He is carrying a *few* dollars in his wallet.

24. The class is full because _____ students are here.

25. A _____ students are scratching their heads.

26. He is changing _____ money.

27. We study _____ lessons each week.

Dictation/Cloze

Listen as your teacher reads, and write the words that you hear in the blanks.

If you _____ _____ around your class _____,
       1   2   3

you _____ probably _____ that the _____ in
   4   5   6

the class _____ _____ different things. Perhaps
       7   8

_____ students _____ _____ their
  9   10   11

_____. Other students _____ _____ their _____.
 12   13   14   15

_____ others _____ _____ because they
 16   17   18

are tired. What _____ you _____ now? Maybe you
           19   20

_____ _____ something funny. For example, perhaps you
 21   22

_____ _____ your _____ or _____
 23   24   25   26

your _____ or _____ with your _____!
    27   28   29

Reading Comprehension

WHAT IS THE *MAIN IDEA?*

The main idea of a reading passage is its *most important idea*, or the *principal idea*. If we really understand the meaning of what we read, we will know the main idea. We can recognize it without difficulty.

What is the main idea of the reading passage "What Is Everybody Doing Now?"

1. The main idea of this reading passage is:
   a. Students yawn because they are tired.
   b. Some students never pay attention to their studies.
   c. Students always pay attention to their studies.
   d. Students make many gestures while they are paying attention to their studies or thinking about something else.

WHAT IS A *DETAIL?*

A detail of a reading passage is an *example or a point which helps to explain or support* the main idea. If we know the main idea of a reading passage, we can also know the details or examples that support the main idea.

What is a detail of the reading passage "What Is Everybody Doing Now?"

2. A detail of this reading passage is:
   a. Students must always pay attention in class.
   b. Some people make very few gestures.
   c. Some students chew their fingernails.
   d. Some students chew their pencils without noticing what they are doing.

FURTHER QUESTIONS ABOUT THE READING PASSAGE

3. According to the reading passage, which of the following sentences is true?
   a. Sometimes students scratch their stomachs while they do their work.
   b. Students don't always pay attention to their body movements.
   c. Students often pull their toes while they listen to their teacher.
   d. Students cover their ears when they listen to their teacher.

4. Which of the following sentences is *not* true according to the reading passage?
   a. Students sometimes rub their eyes while they are studying.
   b. Students sometimes touch their chins.

    c. When students are paying attention to their studies, they are usually not paying attention to their gestures.

    d. Most people squeeze their ankles when they yawn.

5. Which pair has the words that are most similar in meaning?
   a. *most of* and *a few*
   b. *several* and *a few*
   c. *around* and *between*
   d. *stretching* and *scratching*

Guessing Meanings from Context

When we read in a foreign language, we usually do not understand every word. Sometimes it is possible to guess the meaning of a word by looking at the other words in the sentence. We call this procedure *guessing meanings from context*. We can use the information in the sentence to help us understand the meaning of the new word.

    Look at the sentence from the reading "What Is Everybody Doing Now?" Guess the meaning of the italicized word from the context. Circle the letter of the word or words that are most similar in meaning to the italicized word(s).

Example

When people are not paying attention to their gestures, we can sometimes *catch* them doing funny things.

In this sentence, the word *catch* means:
a. think
b. opposite of throw
ⓒ see
d. change

Now guess the meanings of the italicized words below from the context.

1. If we look around our class, we can *observe* students making different gestures.
   a. stop
   b. feel

    c. listen
    d. notice

2. After we walk for a long time, it is a good idea to *massage* our feet and legs.
    a. scratch
    b. chew
    c. jump
    d. rub

3. The students are paying attention while their *instructor* is teaching.
    a. father
    b. classmates
    c. teacher
    d. desk

4. He is learning many new things from his *research* on that subject.
    a. gestures or body movements
    b. cat
    c. studies of new information
    d. rubbing

5. When people are angry, they sometimes *fold* their arms.
    a. pull
    b. chew
    c. cross
    d. scratch

6. She is *folding* the towels and putting them into the closet.
    a. rubbing
    b. doubling
    c. studying
    d. reading

7. *Most likely*, he is yawning because he is tired.
    a. why
    b. good
    c. love
    d. probably

8. She is *squeezing* an orange to make juice.
    a. throwing
    b. rubbing

    c. stretching and pushing
    d. holding very tightly; applying force

Group Activities

SIMON SAYS

Listen as your teacher tells you to make the various body movements mentioned in this chapter. Make the gestures in answer to your teacher's commands, but only if he or she first says the words *Simon says*. If a student makes the gesture when the command is not preceded by the words *Simon says*, he or she must sit down. The last student to remain standing is the winner. Students may also take turns playing the teacher's *Simon* role.

    Some possible commands to use in *Simon Says* are:

Fold your arms.
Rub your eyes.
Pull your ears.
Yawn.
Cover your mouth.

SMALL GROUP CHARADES

Work with a small group of students (three or four). Each student in your group can pantomime gestures mentioned in this chapter. The other students in the group can write the action they see. After every student has pantomimed, students in the group can compare their written answers.

LARGE GROUP CHARADES

One student goes to the front of the room. The teacher gives the student a card with a gesture written on it. The student pantomimes the gesture. The other students guess the gesture and write it. After several students have pantomimed gestures for the class, members of the class can compare answers.

TEAM CHARADES

Divide the class into two teams. The teacher performs the gestures mentioned in the chapter. The students on each team take turns guessing the actions. The team that has the most correct guesses wins.

DICTIONARY EXERCISE

Work with one or two other students, preferably who speak the same native language. Think of other gestures that people make which are not mentioned in this chapter. Look up these words in your bilingual dictionary and report the new English words to the rest of the class.

chapter 2

How Much Do You Touch?

The Simple Present Tense

Pre-reading Questions

What are the people in the different pictures doing?

Where are the people in the first and second pictures? Are they inside or outside?

Is it usual to see people in your country doing these things?

How Much Do You Touch?

Do people in your country hug and kiss on the street? In some countries, it is common for people to show affection in public places.[1] In the United States, for example, we often see couples (two people) hold hands, "make out" or "neck" on the street, in the park, in restaurants, and even on trains and buses![2] But in some other countries, people never show affection in public places because their customs don't permit this. For example, in Korea and Mainland China, custom forbids people to display affection in public places.[3] So, when Korean and Mainland Chinese people visit the United States, they sometimes feel very surprised and even shocked when they see Americans hug and kiss on the street because their own cultures don't allow such conduct.[4]

In some countries, friends show physical affection to each other.[5] In some South American countries, female friends walk arm in arm when they walk along the street together.[6] In Italy and Russia, male friends often kiss each other on both cheeks when they greet.[7] In most cultures, men don't kiss or hug when they greet one another.[8] They usually shake hands or pat each other on the back.[9]

People around the world vary in the amount, manner, and situations in which they touch each other.[10]

1. What is common in some countries?
2. What do we often see in the United States? In what public places do people show affection?
3. Why don't people show affection in public places in Korea and Mainland China?
4. How do Korean and Mainland Chinese people sometimes feel when they visit the United States?
5. What do friends do in some countries?
6. What do female friends do in some South American countries?
7. What do male friends do in Italy and Russia?
8. Do male friends in most cultures kiss and hug when they greet each other?
9. What do they usually do when they greet each other?
10. Are people around the world the same in the amount, manner, and situations in which they touch each other?

The Simple Present Tense

We use the simple present tense to describe actions that happen repeatedly (sometimes, often, usually, always, every day, every week, every month, every year, etc.) or to describe states of being that are generally true.

subject	(frequency adverb)	present tense verb	object
I (you, we, they)	(sometimes)	see	you.
He (she, it)	(often)	sees	me.

To form a question, we put the correct form of the verb *do* at the beginning of our sentence, and we use the infinitive form of the main verb:

form of *do*	subject	(frequency adverb)	infinitive verb	object
Do	I (you, we, they)	(sometimes)	see	you?
Does	he (she, it)	(often)	see	me?

To make a negative sentence, we put the correct form of *do* and the word *not* between the subject and the main verb:

subject	form of *do*	*not*	infinitive verb	object
I (you, we, they)	do	not	see	you.
He (she, it)	does	not	see	me.

Usually, we put *do*, (or *does*) and *not* together to make the following contractions:

do + not = don't   does + not = doesn't

Vocabulary

Write the appropriate verbs in the spaces provided. Do not use the same word more than one time.

feel	hug, embrace	shake
forbid	**kiss**	show, display
greet	pat	vary
hold	permit, allow	visit

Example

a. Some people __kiss__ on both cheeks when they __greet__ each other.

1. In most cultures, male friends _____ hands.

2. In some countries, female friends _____ affection in public.

3. The customs of some cultures _____ displays of affection in public.

4. People from Korea and Mainland China sometimes _____ surprised and even shocked when they _____ the United States.

5. In many countries, men often _____ each other on the back.

6. In some countries, it is common to see couples _____ hands in public.

7. People in different countries _____ in the manner and situations in which they touch each other.

Now supply the appropriate noun:

affection	country(ies)	male(s)	restaurant(s)
amount	couple(s)	manner	situation(s)
bus(es)	culture(s)	park(s)	street(s)
cheek(s)	custom(s)	public place(s)	train(s)
conduct	female(s)		

Example
b. Kissing and hugging are ways to show *affection*.

8. In many countries, it is common to see _____ hold hands.

9. Parks and restaurants are examples of _____.

10. Some cultures permit public affection, but others forbid this kind of _____.

11. In some countries, people kiss on both _____ when they greet each other.

12. In the summer, it's nice to take a walk in the _____ and on the _____.

13. In the United States, usually males and _____ study together in the same class.

14. In American culture, it is a _____ to celebrate Thanksgiving each year in November.

Now supply the appropriate expression:

arm in arm   **in public**
each other, one another   make out, neck

> **Example**
> c. In the United States, couples often kiss *in public* .

15. Parents and children sometimes kiss _____ before they say "good night."

16. Some cultures believe that it's not polite to _____ in public places.

17. That couple always walks _____ along the street.

Now write the appropriate preposition in the space provided. You may use each word more than once.

at   **in**   on

> **Example**
> d. *In* some countries, people embrace openly.

18. We often sit _____ the park.

19. They usually eat _____ a restaurant.

20. _____ Sunday, the family walks along the avenue together.

21. Every day, many people sit _____ buses and trains.

22. We begin classes _____ September.

23. My classes begin _____ September 6 _____ 8:30.

Dictation/Cloze

Listen as your teacher reads, and write the words that you hear in the blanks:

_____ some countries, people _____,
         1   2

_____, and _____ hands in public places. For example,
      3   4

_____ the United States, girlfriends and boyfriends sometimes
      5

_____ or _____ _____ the street, _____
      6   7   8   9

parks, and even _____ buses and subways. But other countries
                       10

_____ _____ public affection. For example,
          11   12

_____ Korea and Mainland China, people _____ _____
      13   14   15

_____ the street. They _____ _____ in restau-
      16   17   18

rants. Public affection _____ _____ their custom. So,
                                 19   20

when Korean and Mainland Chinese people _____ the United
                                                21

States, they sometimes _____ very shocked when they _____
                              22   23

Americans _____ affection _____ public.
                24   25

   In some countries, female friends _____ affection. In South
                                             26

America, female friends _____ arm in arm along the street.
                               27

_____ most countries, male friends usually _____ hands
      28   29

when they _____ each other.
                30

Reading Comprehension

Circle the letter of the correct answers to the following questions:

1. The main idea of this reading passage is:
    a. Chinese people sometimes visit the United States.
    b. Koreans and Americans can never understand each other.
    c. South Americans are more affectionate than North Americans.
    d. Different countries permit different amounts of touching in public.

2. A detail of this reading passage is:
    a. It is not polite to make out in public.
    b. Americans are not polite.
    c. Male friends in Russia sometimes embrace and kiss each other on both cheeks.
    d. Not all Americans like to kiss.

3. According to the reading passage, which of the following sentences is true?
    a. Mainland Chinese people often kiss on the street.
    b. All cultures permit public affection.
    c. The United States forbids couples to make out in public.
    d. In many countries, men shake hands when they greet.

4. Which of the following sentences is *not* true according to the reading passage?
    a. Social customs vary in different countries.
    b. Customs in the United States permit public affection.
    c. Customs in China don't allow public displays of affection.
    d. Women in South America never touch each other.

5. In your opinion, which of the following sentences is probably true?
    a. Korean people often kiss and hug on the street when they visit the United States.
    b. American people like to kiss and hug Korean people in restaurants.
    c. People all over the world like to kiss their friends.
    d. It can be strange for Americans to see two men kiss on both cheeks.

6. Which pair has the words that are most similar in meaning?
    a. *common* and *usual*
    b. *often* and *sometimes*
    c. *never* and *forbid*
    d. *kiss* and *hug*

Guessing Meanings from Context

Guess the meanings of the italicized words from the context. Circle the letter of the word or words that are most similar in meaning to the italicized word(s).

Example

People in different cultures *vary* in the amount they touch each other.
a. surprised
b. affection
ⓒ are different
d. greet

1. In every culture in the world, people *grin* when they feel happy.
   a. cry
   b. talk
   c. clap
   d. smile

2. When people like a concert or play, they usually *applaud*.
   a. sing
   b. scratch their heads
   c. clap their hands
   d. squeeze their fingers

3. When a mother sits down, she often holds her child on her *lap*.
   a. shoulder
   b. nose
   c. chin
   d. knees and thighs

4. An angry mother sometimes *slaps* a child with her hand.
   a. hits
   b. hugs
   c. kisses
   d. rubs

5. When a person is in a bad *mood*, he or she usually doesn't smile.
   a. book
   b. state of mind, or feeling
   c. food
   d. study

6. When something is funny, people often *laugh*.
   a. hold hands
   b. shake hands
   c. opposite of *cry*
   d. kiss

7. When American people greet each other on the street, they often raise their hands and *wave.*
    a. punch
    b. fight
    c. move the open hand quickly from side to side
    d. move the open hand up and down

8. People often run when they are *in a hurry.*
    a. tired
    b. in a bad mood
    c. want to do things fast
    d. happy

9. When a person has a problem, she sometimes *worries.*
    a. laughs
    b. grins
    c. is in a hurry
    d. is preoccupied, thinks nervously about something

10. Cake has a large *amount* of sugar in it.
    a. big
    b. ice cream
    c. dessert
    d. quantity

Word Forms

What is a *word form?*

Many words in English have different forms. There are verb forms, adverb forms, noun forms, and adjective forms.

An adjective is a word that describes a noun. Adjective forms can have many different endings. These endings are also called *suffixes.* The adjective forms below have two different suffixes, *-ed* and *-ing* (don't confuse these with verb endings). Sometimes, an adjective can have an *-ed* suffix when it describes a *feeling* or *emotion.* An adjective can have an *-ing* suffix when it describes a *quality* of something. For example:

> Some Korean and Mainland Chinese people feel *shocked*
> (feeling of
> the people)

> because they think the conduct of Americans is *shocking.*
> (quality of
> the conduct)

Now supply the correct adjective forms in the sentences below:

1. **interested, interesting**

    The students feel _____ because the story is _____.

2. **bored, boring**

   The people feel _____ because the movie is _____.

3. **irritated, irritating**

   Because the loud noise is _____, the children feel

   _____.

4. **confused, confusing**

   The students are _____ because the lesson is

   _____.

5. **tired, tiring**

   They are _____ because the work is _____.

6. **surprised, surprising**

   Because the news is very _____, we feel very

   _____.

7. **annoyed, annoying**

   The parents are _____ because the child's conduct is

   _____.

8. **frightened, frightening**

   The children are _____ because the story is very

   _____.

9. **fascinated, fascinating**

   The audience is _____ because Jimmy's piano playing is

   _____.

REMEMBER: The adjective suffix *-ing* describes a quality. The adjective suffix *-ed* describes an emotion.

Group Activities

SIMON SAYS

Listen as your teacher tells you to make the various body movements mentioned in both this chapter and the last chapter. Make the gestures your teacher tells you to, but only if he or she first says the words *Simon says*. If you make a mistake and make the gesture when the command is not preceded by the words *Simon says,* you must sit down and stop playing the game. The last person left standing is the winner.

Some possible commands to use in *Simon Says* are:

Shake hands with the person next to you.
Pat your neighbor on the back.
Look surprised.
Look shocked.

ROLE-PLAYS

Work alone or with one or two other students from your native country.
Choose one of the following situations. Show the rest of the class the
conduct of a person from your culture if he or she:

sees a brother for the first time in two years.

sees a sister for the first time in two years.

is saying goodbye to his or her mother at the airport, and will not see
her again for one year.

is walking along the street and meets an instructor from the
university.

is walking along the street and meets a friend.

is walking along the street and meets a child he or she knows.

is walking along the street and sees an attractive man or woman.

is walking along the street and sees a couple embracing and kissing.

LARGE GROUP CHARADES

Pairs of students may take turns going to the front of the classroom. The
teacher gives each pair of students a card with an action written on it (for
example, "shake hands," "walk arm in arm," etc.). These students perform the actions, and the others in the class write them. After several pairs
of students have pantomimed actions for the class, the other members of
the class may compare their answers.

SMALL GROUP CHARADES

Work with a small group of students (three or four). Pairs of students in
your group can take turns pantomiming gestures mentioned in this chapter (shaking hands, patting on the back, etc.). The other students in the
group can write the actions they see. After each pair of students in the
group has pantomimed, students in the group may compare their written
answers.

SMALL GROUP DISCUSSION

Work with a small group of students. Each student in your group can
describe the customs for public touching in his or her country. One student
should write the customs that the other students describe. Later, this
student can report the customs to the rest of the class.

 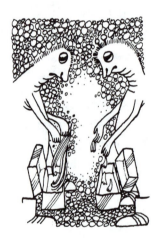 

chapter 3

The Story of Betty and Barney Hill

The Simple Past Tense

Pre-reading Questions

Look at each picture. Tell what you see in each one.
What is a U.F.O.? What is a flying saucer? What is a spaceman?

The Story of Betty and Barney Hill

Betty and Barney Hill were a married couple who lived in New Hampshire.[1] They both told an incredible story. Some people believe their story and some people don't. See what you think about it.[2]

One night, Betty and Barney were driving through the woods, when suddenly a flying saucer landed in front of their car.[3] Two very strange-looking spacemen came out of the flying saucer.[4] They took Betty and Barney into their spaceship.[5] These spacemen examined them.[6] They took sample pieces of skin and hair from the bodies of the couple.[7] Then they put these samples into special glass cases.[8] Betty and Barney felt very afraid, but the spacemen didn't hurt them.[9] They released Betty and Barney after they examined them.[10]

This experience upset the couple very much. It shook them up.[11] They went to a psychiatrist for help.[12] The psychiatrist hypnotized them,[13] and they told their story under hypnosis.[14] In most cases, people tell the truth under hypnosis.[15]

1. Who were Betty and Barney Hill? Where did they live?
2. What do they both tell? Does everyone believe their story?
3. What happened one night?
4. Who came out of the flying saucer?
5. Where did they take Betty and Barney?
6. What did the spacemen do to Betty and Barney?
7. What did they take from the bodies of the couple?
8. Where did they put these samples?
9. How did Betty and Barney feel? Did the spacemen hurt them?
10. What did the spacemen do after they examined Betty and Barney?
11. What did this experience do to the couple?
12. Where did the couple go for help?
13. What did the psychiatrist do?
14. What did they do under hypnosis?
15. Do people usually tell the truth under hypnosis?
16. Do you believe the incredible story of Betty and Barney Hill?

The Simple Past Tense

We use the simple past tense of a verb to describe an action that happened at a point in the past. The simple past tense may have a *regular* or *irregular* form:

Regular form:

subject	verb + -ed	object
I (you, he, she, it, we, they)	helped	them.

Irregular form:

subject	irregular past form	object
I (you, he, she, it, we, they)	told	them.

To make a question in the simple past tense, we put *did* (the past tense form of *do*) at the beginning of our sentence, and we use the infinitive form of the main verb:

did	subject	infinitive main verb	object
Did	I (you, he, she, it, we, they)	help	them?
Did	I (you, he, she, it, we, they)	tell	them?

To make a negative sentence, we put *did* and the word *not* between the subject and the main verb:

subject	*did not*	infinitive main verb	object
I (you, he, she, it, we, they)	did not	help	them.
I (you, he, she, it, we, they)	did not	tell	them.

Usually, we put *did* and *not* together to form the following contraction:

did + not = didn't

It can be difficult to remember the past tense forms of all the irregular verbs. The *irregular verb rhyme* below can help you remember some of the most common ones. It is even more helpful if you say the rhyme in 4/4 (musical) time, and snap your fingers after you say each verb. For example:

present	past
I think [snap fingers] →	I thought [snap fingers]
I buy [snap]	→ I bought [snap]

irregular verb rhyme

I think—I thought	I say—I said	I drive—I drove
I buy—I bought	I read—I read	I choose—I chose
I bring—I brought	I lead—I led	I freeze—I froze
I teach—I taught	I feed—I fed	I rise—I rose
I catch—I caught		

I write—I wrote	I grow—I grew	I go—I went
I speak—I spoke	I fly—I flew	I send—I sent
I break—I broke	I know—I knew	I lend—I lent
I wake—I woke	I blow—I blew	I bend—I bent
	I throw—I threw	I mean—I meant
I sleep—I slept		
I keep—I kept	I can—I could	I hit—I hit
I leave—I left	I stand—I stood	I hurt—I hurt
		I put—I put

Vocabulary

Write the appropriate past tense verbs in the spaces provided:

believed (believe)	hypnotized (hypnotize)	shook up (shake up)
came out (come out)	**landed** (land)	told (tell)
drove (drive)	lived (live)	took (take)
examined (examine)	put (put)	upset (upset)
felt (feel)	released (release)	went (go)
hurt (hurt)		

Example

a. The airplane ___*landed*___ in the airport at 9:00 P.M. last night.

1. We _____ our car from New York to California.

2. The psychiatrist _____ Betty and Barney Hill.

3. The man _____ his leg in a sports accident last week.

4. The doctor _____ many patients at the hospital today.

5. I _____ to the doctor because I didn't feel well.

6. The teacher _____ the students when the class ended.

7. The car accident _____ him _____ very much.

8. We _____ our books inside our bookcase.

9. She _____ very happy last weekend.

10. The students _____ of the school after their class.

Now supply the appropriate noun:

body (bodies)	psychiatrist(s)	story (stories)
case(s)	spaceman **(spacemen)**	truth
flying saucer(s)	spaceship(s)	woods
piece(s)	skin	

Example

b. Betty and Barney felt afraid of the *Spacemen*.

11. Some people believe the ＿＿＿＿＿ of Betty and Barney Hill, and some people don't.

12. In the ＿＿＿＿＿ we can find many different trees and flowers.

13. Astronauts travel to outer space in a ＿＿＿＿＿.

14. He wanted another ＿＿＿＿＿ of cake.

15. She went to a ＿＿＿＿＿ because she had an emotional problem.

16. He always told the ＿＿＿＿＿ because he was an honest person.

17. At the museum, we can see many valuable objects inside glass

＿＿＿＿＿.

18. Sometimes, strong sunlight can change the color of our

＿＿＿＿＿.

Now write the appropriate preposition or prepositional phrase in the space provided. You may use each word more than once.

about   for   in front of   **into**   under

Example

c. At the beginning of class, the students walked *into* the classroom.

19. They went to the store ＿＿＿＿＿ milk.

20. He didn't want to think ＿＿＿＿＿ his problems.

21. The teacher sat ＿＿＿＿＿ the classroom.

22. The mouth is _____ the nose.

23. Betty and Barney told the truth _____ hypnosis.

24. It is dangerous to drive _____ the influence of alcohol.

Dictation/Cloze

Listen as your teacher reads, and write the words that you hear in the blanks:

Certainly, Betty and Barney Hill _____ expect to see any
_____1_____

_____ or _____ when they _____ through the
_____2_____   _____3_____   _____4_____

_____ that night. So, of course they _____ very surprised
_____5_____   _____6_____

and shocked when a _____ saucer suddenly _____
_____7_____   _____8_____

in front of their car. They were even more shocked when the spacemen

_____ them into the spaceship and _____ them. Natu-
_____9_____   _____10_____

rally, the _____ felt afraid when the spacemen _____
_____11_____   _____12_____

sample _____ of their _____ and hair. Surely they
_____13_____   _____14_____

_____ relieved when the spacemen finally _____ them.
_____15_____   _____16_____

Of course this experience _____ the husband and wife very much.
_____17_____

For this reason, they _____ to a _____. At first, the doctor
_____18_____   _____19_____

_____ _____ the couple's _____ was true. He
_____20_____ _____21_____   _____22_____

hypnotized them to find out the _____. After Betty and Barney
_____23_____

_____ the same story _____ hypnosis, the doctor
_____24_____   _____25_____

_____ know what to _____!
_____26_____   _____27_____

Reading Comprehension

Circle the letter of the correct answers to the following questions:

1. The main idea of this reading passage is:
   a. Betty and Barney Hill didn't tell the truth about their experience.
   b. Flying saucers and spacemen don't exist.
   c. Betty and Barney Hill tell an incredible story of their experience with a flying saucer.
   d. Psychiatrists often put their patients under hypnosis.

2. A detail of this reading passage is:
   a. Most people don't believe in flying saucers.
   b. People in many parts of the world see spacemen and spaceships.
   c. Spacemen examined Betty and Barney Hill.
   d. Psychiatrists always hypnotize their patients.

3. According to the reading passage, which of the following sentences is true?
   a. Betty and Barney Hill told their story under hypnosis.
   b. Everybody believes Betty and Barney Hill's story.
   c. Betty and Barney Hill were from California.
   d. Betty and Barney Hill weren't afraid when they saw the flying saucer.

4. Which of the following sentences is *not* true according to the reading passage?
   a. Some people believe Betty and Barney Hill's story and some people don't.
   b. Betty and Barney Hill were driving their car through the woods.
   c. A spaceman wanted to marry Betty Hill.
   d. The spacemen permitted Betty and Barney to leave after they examined them.

5. In your opinion, which of the following sentences is probably true?
   a. Betty and Barney Hill didn't like psychiatrists.
   b. Betty and Barney Hill felt very, very surprised when they saw the flying saucer.
   c. Betty and Barney Hill forgot their experience quickly.
   d. Betty and Barney Hill felt happy and calm when they saw the spaceship in front of their car.

6. Which pair has the words that are most similar in meaning?
   a. *married* and *couple*
   b. *flying saucer* and *airplane*
   c. *release* and *keep*
   d. *hurt* and *cause pain*

Guessing Meanings from Context

Guess the meanings of the italicized words from the context. Circle the letter of the word or words that are most similar in meaning to the italicized word(s):

> **Example**
>
> Betty and Barney Hill told an *incredible* story.
> **a.** not true
> **b.** beautiful
> ©. difficult to believe, very surprising
> **d.** very interesting, but not true

1. In the sentence, "see what you think about it," the word *see* means:
   a. watch
   b. decide
   c. look
   d. hear

2. Like Betty and Barney Hill, people in many parts of the world report seeing *UFOs*.
   a. psychiatrists
   b. ugly flying objects
   c. cars
   d. unidentified flying objects

3. He never told the truth. He *told lies* all the time.
   a. didn't agree
   b. didn't tell the truth
   c. said stupid things
   d. told stories about spaceships

4. We were sitting in the sun at the beach, when *suddenly* it began to rain.
   a. cloud
   b. ocean
   c. without expecting it, unexpectedly
   d. not surprisingly

5. At the zoo, we were surprised to see so many *strange-looking* birds.
   a. different and unusual looking
   b. common and normal looking
   c. stupid
   d. attractive

6. Betty and Barney Hill felt *scared* of the spacemen.
   a. angry
   b. afraid
   c. love
   d. happy

7. People in many parts of the world tell *tales* of their experiences with UFO's.
   a. the truth
   b. stories
   c. spacemen
   d. flying saucers

8. A *flying saucer* landed in front of Betty and Barney Hill's car.
   a. an airplane
   b. a round, flying object
   c. a truck
   d. a bird

9. Very often people put *saucers* under their coffee cups.
   a. sugar
   b. small plates
   c. fingers
   d. milk

10. Betty and Barney Hill's story is certainly *amazing*.
    a. stupid
    b. boring
    c. incredible
    d. usual

Verb Forms

Write the correct past tense forms of the irregular verbs in the spaces provided. Try not to look at the *irregular verb rhyme* until you have finished.

Example

Betty and Barney Hill __*went*__ to a psychiatrist.
(go)

1. Betty and Barney Hill _____ a spaceship.
   (see)

2. They _____ to a psychiatrist about their experience.
   (speak)

3. We _____ our car across the country last summer.
   (drive)

4. The students _____ their notebooks to class.
   (bring)

5. The teacher _____ an important lesson yesterday.
   (teach)

6. The small shoes _____ his big feet.
   (hurt)

7. The students _____ the story in chapter one.
   (read)

Group Activities

SMALL GROUP RETELLING AND DISCUSSION

1. Work with a small group of students. Each student in the group can tell a little of the Betty and Barney Hill story until the entire story has been retold. After that, each student can give his or her opinion of the story. Does each student believe Betty and Barney Hill's story or not? One student in the group should write the opinions of each student, and later report them to the rest of the class.

2. Did you or someone you know have an experience with a UFO? If so, tell the rest of the class about this experience. When you finish telling your story, the rest of the class will write about it.

ROLE-PLAY

Divide the class into small groups. Each group can choose one of the following situations to role-play for the rest of the class:

1. Write a dialogue between Betty and Barney Hill and the spacemen. Then, role-play this situation for the rest of the class.

2. Write a dialogue between Betty and Barney Hill and their psychiatrist. Then, role-play this situation for the rest of the class.

3. Imagine another situation where some people see a UFO. Write a dialogue and role-play the situation for the rest of the class.

SIMON SAYS

Listen as your teacher tells you to act out various emotions. If your teacher first says the words *Simon says*, then you act out the emotion. If your teacher does *not* say the words *Simon says* first, then you *do not* act out the emotion. For example, if your teacher says, "Simon says, look afraid," then you look afraid. But if your teacher says only, "Look afraid," then you don't do anything. If you make a mistake, you must sit down. The last student left standing is the winner.

Some possible commands to use in *Simon Says* are:

Look shocked.   Look angry.
Look surprised.   Look confused.
Look happy.   Look worried.
Look sad.

Skimming and Scanning

WHAT IS *SKIMMING*?

When we *skim* a reading passage, an article, or a book, we don't read every word. We look through it quickly until we know the main idea, or the general idea, of the text. (Often, the main idea is in the first sentence or the first few sentences of the reading.) For example, when we read a newspaper, we usually don't read every word of every article; instead, we look through the newspaper and skim some articles to get their general idea.

Look at the reading below. Don't read every word of it. Just skim it until you know its main idea:

The UFO Incident

The American public was fascinated[a] by Betty and Barney Hill's story of their 1961 meeting with the spacemen. Interest in their story continued over the years,[b] and in 1975, American television producers[c] made a movie about the couple's experience. The name of the movie was *The UFO Incident*. Two very fine American actors played the roles[d] of the famous husband and wife: James Earl Jones played the part[e] of Barney Hill, and Estelle Parsons played the part of Betty Hill. Many Americans watched *The UFO Incident* on TV with great interest. No doubt, stories of UFO's and space will continue to fascinate the American public and inspire movie-makers.

After we skim a reading, we can write the main idea of it in one or two sentences. For example:

American television producers made a movie of the

---

[a]very, very interested   [b]*over the years:* for several or many years   [c]persons who make programs for television   [d]characters   [e]role

Betty and Barney Hill story called The UFO Incident.
The American public was very interested in the story.

Now we can *scan* the reading for more specific information, or details.

WHAT IS *SCANNING?*

When we *scan* an article, a book, or a reading, we don't read every word. We look through the text quickly until we find specific information or details that we want to know. We have a certain question, and we look for the answer. For example, if we want to know in what theater a certain movie is showing, we scan the newspaper until we find this information. It's not necessary for us to read every word and line of the newspaper. It's necessary only to look through it quickly until we find the specific information that we want.

Scan "The UFO Incident" for the following information:

1. In what year did Betty and Barney Hill have their meeting with the spacemen?

   _____

2. In what year did television producers make the movie *The UFO Incident?*

   _____

3. What was the name of the actress who played the role of Betty Hill?

   _____

4. What was the name of the actor who played the part of Barney Hill?

   _____

5. Who watched the UFO incident?

   _____

Now look at the reading below. First, skim it for the main idea:

Great American Science Fiction Films: *ET*

Americans love science fiction[a] movies. Such[b] interest is not surprising in a country that sends spaceships and astronauts[c] to outer space.[d] The four American films that made the most money (or had the biggest box office[e] sales[f]) were all in the science fiction category: *ET, Star Wars, The Return of the Jedi,* and *The Empire Strikes Back.* The 1982 film *ET* made more money than any other movie in motion picture^g history. It grossed^h almost three hundred sixty million dollars from box office sales in the United States and Canada. North Americans of all ages—both children and adults—loved *ET.*

People in many other countries also loved *ET.* The film was a great international success.^{i} Movie theaters around the world requested^j *ET* more often than any other film in history.

In our present space age,^{k} science fiction films fascinate movie-goers^l everywhere.

Write the main idea of the reading in one or two sentences:

_____

_____

Now scan the reading for the following information:

1. Why is American interest in science fiction not surprising?

   _____

2. Name the four American films that made the most money at the box office.

   _____

3. How much money did *ET* gross? In what countries?

   _____

4. In what year did the film *ET* come out?

   _____

5. Did any other film make more money than *ET?*

   _____

6. Was *ET* popular only in North America?

   _____

7. What age group liked *ET?*

   _____

^{a} stories (that are not true) that include real or imagined science and its influence on persons or the world ^{b}*such* interest = interest *like this* ^{c}people who travel away from the earth to outer space ^{d}outside the earth's (our planet's) atmosphere ^{e}an office (at a theater) that sells tickets ^{f}the selling of something ^{g}movie, film ^{h}earned in total from ticket sales at the box office ^{i}achievement having a good or excellent result ^{j}asked for ^{k}our time of exploration of outer space ^{l}people who go to the movies

chapter 4

A Funny Incident

The Simple Past Tense

Pre-reading Questions

Do different words in English sometimes sound the same to you? (for example, *color* and *collar, thing* and *sing, were* and *where*)

Do you sometimes have problems understanding English for this reason?

Did you ever have a funny experience because you confused two different words in English?

Look at the picture and read (or listen to) the story.

In this reading, an American girl named Sally describes a funny experience she had in Spain because of her difficulties with the Spanish language.

A Funny Incident

A funny thing happened to me when I was in Spain.[1] Two Spanish words sounded the same to my American ears. These words were *sangria* and *sonrie*. *Sangria* is a type of wine. *Sonrie* means *smile*.[2]

One day, a man came to visit at our house.[3] He looked at my shy, serious face, and said, "Sonrie, por favor." ("Smile, please.")[4] But I understood, "Sangria, please." I thought the man wanted a glass of sangria.[5]

"Now?" I asked him.

"Of course now," he answered.

"Sure," I said to him. "One moment." I went to the kitchen and returned with some sangria and two glasses.[6]

The man looked confused. "Do Americans have to drink sangria before they can smile?" he asked.[7] But I misunderstood his question. I thought the man asked, "Do Americans drink sangria?"[8]

"They certainly do," I said.[9]

"How crazy Americans are!" the man said.

And we were both very confused as we drank our sangria.[10]

1. What happened to Sally when she was in Spain?
2. What two Spanish words sounded the same to her "American ears"? What do these words mean?
3. What happened one day?
4. What did the man say to Sally?
5. What did Sally *think* the man said to her?
6. What did Sally do?
7. What did the man say to Sally when she returned with the sangria and two glasses?
8. What did she *think* the man said to her?
9. What did she answer?
10. How did Sally and the man feel as they drank their sangria?

Vocabulary

Write the appropriate past tense forms of the verbs in the spaces provided. Do not use the same word more than one time.

answer	come	happen	say	think
ask	drink	look	smile	understand
be (was, were)	**go**	misunderstand	sound	

Examples

a. Sally _went_____ to the kitchen for some sangria and two glasses.

b. The man _asked_____ Sally, "Do Americans have to drink sangria before they can smile?"

1. We _____ a lot of sangria in the Spanish restaurant last night.

2. He _____ Spanish very well when he was a child, but now he understands very little.

3. They _____ nervous about speaking a foreign language.

4. After he told us in English, he _____ the same thing to our friends in Spanish.

5. I _____ you when you said you were angry. I thought you said you were hungry.

6. The teacher _____ all the students' questions in class that morning.

7. My friend _____ to class late yesterday.

8. The beautiful music _____ wonderful.

9. The United States _____ two hundred years old in 1976.

10. She looked happy and _____ when she heard the good news.

11. What _____ to him? He doesn't look well.

12. We _____ he was crazy, but we didn't tell him that.

Now supply the appropriate noun:

    glass   **kitchen**   smile   type   wine

Example

c. We ate breakfast in the _kitchen_____.

13. They always drink _____ with dinner.
14. That child has a very happy _____ on his face.
15. Ice cream and cake are _____ of desserts.
16. He drank a _____ of milk every day.

Supply the appropriate noun from this list for rooms of a house.

attic   basement   bedroom   dining room   living room

17. We eat dinner in the _____.
18. We sleep in the _____.
19. He puts old furniture down in the _____.
20. She puts old clothes and photographs up in the _____.
21. After dinner, we talk, read, play games and watch television in the

_____.

Now write the appropriate preposition. If no preposition is necessary, write an "X" in the space. You may use the same preposition more than one time.

at   in   of   **to**

Examples
d. A funny thing happened __*to*__ Sally.

e. He asked __X__ his friend to help him.

22. We looked _____ all the beautiful buildings _____ the city.
23. All the dresses looked _____ beautiful.
24. An apple is a type _____ fruit.
25. He came _____ tell us something important.
26. A lot _____ people live in New York City.
27. "Do your homework," the teacher told _____ the students.
28. "We always do our homework," the students said _____ the teacher.

Dictation/Cloze

Listen as your teacher reads, and write the words that you hear in the blank spaces:

When Sally _____ in Spain, a funny thing _____ to
            1   2

her. She confused two words that _____ the same to her American
                                          3

ears. These words _____ *sangria* and *sonrie.* One day, a man
                        4

_____ to visit at her house. The man _____ Sally
        5   6

_____ very serious. He _____ to her, "Sonrie, por
        7   7a

favor." ("Smile, please.") But Sally _____ _____. She thought
                                          8   9

the man _____, "Sangria, please." So, Sally _____ to
              10   11

the kitchen and _____ with some sangria and two glasses.
                      12

The man _____ confused. He _____, "Do Americans
              13   14

have to drink sangria before they can smile?" But again Sally _____
                                                                    15

him. She _____ he _____, "Do Americans drink
              16   17

sangria?" "They certainly do," Sally _____. Then the man _____
                                          18   19

that Americans _____ even more crazy than he _____.
                    20   21

Both he and Sally _____ very confused as they _____
                        22   23

their sangria.

Reading Comprehension

Circle the letter of the correct answers to the following questions:

1. The main idea of this reading passage is:
   a. Americans can't learn a foreign language.
   b. Spanish people think American people are crazy.

   c. Sally had a funny misunderstanding in a foreign language.
   d. People make mistakes when they drink sangria.
2. A detail of this reading passage is:
   a. Sally was a serious person.
   b. Americans like to drink sangria.
   c. The man didn't like sangria.
   d. Two Spanish words sounded the same to Sally's American ears.

3. According to the reading passage, which of the following sentences is true?
   a. Americans have to drink sangria before they can smile.
   b. The man asked Sally for a glass of sangria.
   c. Americans don't drink sangria.
   d. Sally misunderstood the man two times.

4. Which of the following sentences is *not* true according to the reading?
   a. Sally went to the kitchen for sangria and two glasses.
   b. Sally was an American person visiting Spain.
   c. Sally understood some Spanish.
   d. Sally didn't understand one word of Spanish.

5. In your opinion, which of the following sentences is probably true?
   a. Sally spoke Spanish in Spain for many years.
   b. Sally was just beginning to speak and understand Spanish.
   c. The man knew Sally misunderstood him.
   d. The man was in love with Sally.

6. Which pair has the words that are most similar in meaning?
   a. *type* and *wine*
   b. *ask* and *said*
   c. *confused* and *unhappy*
   d. *of course* and *sure*

Guessing Meanings from Context

Guess the meanings of the italicized words from the context. Circle the letter of the word or words that are most similar in meaning to the italicized word(s):

Example

The student left for school in the morning and *returned* home in the evening.
   a. right
   b. tired
   c. came back
   d. house

1. I gave him my pen in the morning, and he *returned* it to me in the afternoon.
   a. lost
   b. came back
   c. kept
   d. gave back

2. The students didn't understand the teacher very well. They *appeared* confused.
   a. saw
   b. understood
   c. looked
   d. unhappy

3. We laughed at the story because it was *funny*.
   a. comical
   b. sad
   c. opposite of "cry"
   d. long

4. We heard a *funny* noise in the woods that night. Nobody understood what it was.
   a. comical
   b. humorous
   c. strange
   d. nose

5. It was difficult to find the museum because we received *confusing* directions.
   a. clear, easy to follow
   b. good
   c. unclear, difficult to understand
   d. correct

6. In some countries, people kiss on *both* cheeks when they greet each other.
   a. two
   b. lips
   c. hug
   d. face

7. Apples are his favorite *type* of fruit.
   a. banana
   b. vegetable
   c. kind
   d. dessert

8. The *shy* child didn't talk to anyone and he looked afraid.
   a. strong
   b. timid
   c. happy
   d. appeared

9. He didn't smile very much. He was a very *serious* person.
   a. comical
   b. important and powerful
   c. happy
   d. not joking or funny

10. He picked up the bottle and *poured* some wine into our glasses.
   a. drank
   b. put
   c. offered
   d. broke

Word Forms

Sometimes, the same word can be a noun or a verb, depending on its position in the sentence. In most cases, a verb follows a noun or a pronoun and is conjugated. Often, before a noun, we find an article (*a, an, the*), a possessive pronoun (*my, your, his, her, our, their*), or an adjective.

Look at the two examples below. In the first sentence, the word *sound* is a verb. In the second sentence, it is a noun:

> The music *sounds* wonderful. (verb)
> The music has a wonderful *sound*. (noun)

In the pairs of sentences below, the same word is used as both a noun and a verb. Identify the italicized words as either nouns or verbs:

Examples

a. He *laughs* all the time. __V__

b. He has a happy *laugh*. __N__

1. She *smiles* a lot. _____

2. She has a pretty *smile*. _____

3. Our family *visits* every Sunday. _____

4. Every Sunday, we have a *visit* from our family. _____

5. We felt happy about his *return*. _____

6. He *returned* home yesterday. _____

7. The student *answered* his question. _____

8. The student gave a correct *answer*. _____

9. He often has a *drink* before dinner. _____

10. He *drinks* a cocktail before dinner. _____

11. This book has a *reading* called "A Funny Incident." _____

12. The students are *reading* "A Funny Incident." _____

Group Activities

ROLE-PLAYS

1. Choose pairs of students to come to the front of the room and act out the story "A Funny Incident."

2. Students can work in groups or pairs and write about original situations in which misunderstandings happen because of English words with similar sounds. Students can act out these situations for the rest of the class.

SMALL GROUP RETELLING OF STORY AND DISCUSSION

Each member of the group can tell a little of the story "A Funny Incident," until the entire story has been retold.

Next, with the members of your group, make a list of pairs of words with similar sounds. When your list is finished, report these words to the rest of the class. The teacher can write the pairs of words on the board and say them aloud, pointing out the differences in sound to the students. For example: *cup* and *cop*.

After students repeat each word the teacher says, they can listen as the teacher uses each one in a sentence and identify which word they hear in the sentence. For example, the teacher can write on the board, and say the words, *Get me a cop* and *Get me a cup*. When students hear the first sentence, they can respond with the word *policeman*. When students hear the second sentence, they can respond with the word *drink*. This activity can be repeated with other words that the students choose.

SIMON SAYS

Listen as your teacher tells you to act out the various emotions and actions mentioned in both this chapter and previous chapters. Act out the emotions and actions only if your teacher first says the words *Simon says*. If you make a mistake, you must stop playing the game. The last person left standing is the winner.

Possible commands are:

Look shy.	Look crazy.	Drink a glass of wine.
Look serious.	Laugh.	Drink a cup of coffee.
Look confused.	Smile.	Spill a cup of coffee.
Look timid.	Pour a glass of wine.	

Watch Those Sounds!

Sometimes it's difficult to hear certain sounds in another language if we don't have those same sounds in our native language. English has many sounds that we often don't find in other languages. The *th* sound is one example. It can be difficult for students of English to hear the *th* sound in words like *three* or *thin*. Often, they hear a *t* or *d* sound instead of a *th*. So, instead of hearing the word *three*, they hear the word *tree*. Instead of hearing *thin*, they hear *tin*[a] or *din*.[b] It's a good idea to *watch* native speakers of English make this sound. Notice how they put the tongue *between* the teeth, *not behind* the teeth. First watch, and then listen to how this sound is different from a *t* or a *d* sound.

English also has many vowel sounds that other languages don't. One of these is the sound we find in the words *but*, *about*, *cup*, and *love*. Students of English often hear these sounds as they hear the *o* in *hot*. This is incorrect. Again, it can be helpful[c] to watch native English speakers make this sound. When they pronounce the vowel sound in *cup* or *love*, they don't open their mouths very much. Also, they don't use the muscles[d] around their mouths very much. These are relaxed.[e] To make the vowel sound in *hot*, the mouth opens more, and so more muscles in the mouth area are used. First watch a native speaker, and then listen.

To learn the sounds of English, we sometimes need to use our eyes as well as[f] our ears.

Skim the reading "Watch Those Sounds!" and write the main idea in one or two sentences. You can work alone or with another student:

_____

_____

[a]kind of metal [b]noise [c]give help [d]parts of the body that enable us to move [e]calm, not moving or tense [f]and also

Now scan the reading for the following information:

1. Can we always hear all the sounds in a foreign language?

    _____

2. Can we find *all* the same sounds in every language?

    _____

3. What sound is sometimes difficult for students of English to hear?
    What other sound do they sometimes hear instead?

    _____

4. What words do students of English sometimes confuse?

    _____

5. What can you do if it's difficult for you to hear the *th* sound?

    _____

6. Where do native speakers of English put their tongue when they
    make the *th* sound? Where *don't* they put their tongue?

    _____

7. What other sounds does English have that other languages don't?

    _____

8. Give an example of one of these sounds. What are some words that
    have this sound?

    _____

9. What other sound do students of English often hear instead of this
    sound?

    _____

10. What can be helpful for students?

    _____

11. How do native speakers of English make the two different sounds?

    _____

12. What do we sometimes need to do to learn the sounds of English?

    _____

chapter 5

Yukio and Cindy

Introduction of Should
Review of the Simple Past Tense

Pre-reading Questions

Did you ever live in a foreign country?

Did you ever feel lonely in a foreign country? Did you miss your home and family?

Did the foreign country feel strange to you sometimes?

Did you ever have a boyfriend or girlfriend from a foreign country?

Look at the pictures. Tell what you see.

Yukio and Cindy

Yukio is a twenty-four year old Japanese businessman.[1] A few months ago, his company sent him to work at its New York City office for a period of half a year.[2] This was Yukio's first experience living in the United States.[3]

Yukio thought New York City was very exciting, but he also found it very strange.[4] It was difficult for him to get accustomed to it.[5] He found it strange to be with people from so many different ethnic groups.[6] He sometimes found American people very direct and outspoken, though at the same time he felt very curious about them.[7] He wished he could become friends with some Americans, but he wasn't sure how to approach them.[8] Most of the time, Yukio felt very lonely and missed Japan.[9]

But soon some sunshine came into his life.[10] A new clerk came to work in his office part-time. She was American, as were most of the clerks in his office. Her name was Cindy.[11] She was intelligent, friendly, and very attractive.[12] Cindy was also a student. She was studying business administration.[13] Cindy and Yukio got along very well. They talked together whenever possible.[14] Cindy told Yukio her dreams of having a successful business career. She said she was not really interested in getting married or having children. She wanted to use all of her energy for her career.[15] Yukio found Cindy very interesting and very different from the women he knew before.[16] Similarly, Cindy found Yukio unique among all the men that she knew.[17] Soon the two fell in love and they were both very happy.[18]

But now it is almost time for Yukio to return to Japan.[19] Yukio wants Cindy to return to Japan with him and marry him.[20] But Cindy doesn't know if it is possible for a woman to pursue a business career in Japan. Also, she doesn't speak any Japanese. She fears that Yukio wants her to become a traditional wife and have children right away.[21] Cindy wants Yukio to stay in New York City.[22] But Yukio is homesick. He still finds New York a very strange place, and he longs to return to Japan.[23]

Yukio and Cindy feel confused and miserable. They don't know what they should do.[24] Should they stay in New York? Should they go to Japan? Sometimes they think they should separate.[25] But they also feel they cannot live without each other.[26]

1. Who is Yukio?
2. What happened a few months ago?
3. Did Yukio live in the United States before?
4. What did Yukio think of New York City?
5. Was it easy for Yukio to get accustomed to New York City?
6. What did Yukio find strange?
7. How did he feel about American people?

8. What did he wish?
9. How did Yukio feel most of the time?
10. What soon happened to Yukio?
11. What was the "sunshine"?
12. What kind of person was Cindy?
13. What did Cindy study?
14. How did Cindy and Yukio get along?
15. What did Cindy tell Yukio?
16. What did Yukio think of Cindy?
17. What did Cindy think of Yukio?
18. What soon happened?
19. What is happening now?
20. What does Yukio want?
21. How does Cindy feel about this?
22. What does Cindy want?
23. How does Yukio feel about this?
24. How do Yukio and Cindy both feel?
25. What do they both think sometimes?
26. What do they both feel?
27. What do you think Yukio and Cindy should do?

Introducing Should

When we put the word *should* before a verb, it means that the action of the verb is *advisable*, or a *good idea:*

subject	should	infinitive verb
I (you, he, she, it, we, they)	should	go.

To form a question, we reverse the position of the subject and *should*:

should	subject	infinitive verb
Should	I (you, he, she, it, we, they)	go?

To form a negative sentence, we put the word *not* after the word *should*:

subject	should not	infinitive verb
I (you, he, she, it, we, they)	should not	go.

Often, we put *should* and *not* together to form the following contraction:

should + not = shouldn't

PRACTICE WITH *SHOULD:* EXPRESSING OPINIONS

Write *should* and the appropriate verbs in the spaces provided. Do not use the same verb more than one time.

become   forget   have   learn   marry   **stay**

Example
a. Perhaps some students in the class think that Yukio and Cindy **should stay** together.

1. Cindy _____ Yukio and go to Japan.
2. Cindy _____ a traditional wife.
3. Cindy _____ children right away. It's better if she becomes a mother when she is young.
4. Cindy _____ to speak Japanese.
5. Cindy _____ her business career in the United States and go to Japan.

Now write the above sentences with *shouldn't* to express the opposite opinion.

Example
b. Yukio and Cindy shouldn't stay together.

6. _____
7. _____
8. _____
9. _____
10. _____

Vocabulary

Now write the appropriate past tense forms of the verbs in the spaces provided. In some sentences, the verbs are negative; in others, they are affirmative.

approach	find	long	wish
fall in love	get along	**miss**	
fear	**know**	pursue	

Examples

c. Yukio *missed* _____ Japan very much.

d. Cindy *didn't know* how to speak Japanese.

11. Yukio and Cindy _____ very well and talked together whenever possible.

12. Soon, Yukio _____ with Cindy and wanted to marry her.

13. Yukio _____ New York a comfortable place to live.

14. Cindy _____ Yukio could stay in New York.

15. In the past, women in most countries _____ careers. They spent their time in the home.

16. A stranger _____ us on the street and asked for directions.

17. The child cried every night because he _____ the dark.

18. After living in another country for a year, she _____ to see her family again.

Now supply the appropriate noun:

administration	children	energy	sunshine
business	clerk	ethnic groups	**wife**
career	dream	period	

Example

e. The couple just got married. Now they are husband and *wife* _____.

19. It's often easy for young _____ to learn a foreign language.

20. The automobile _____ is a big industry in Japan.

21. These days, many women want to work and have interesting _____.

22. When we are tired, we don't have a lot of _____.

23. In English classes, we often have students from many different countries and _____.

24. Since he was a child, his _____ was to visit the United States.

25. It felt good to sit in the warm, bright _____ at the beach.

26. The _____ of the university decided to end classes early the day before the vacation.

Now supply the appropriate adjective:

attractive	homesick	miserable	successful
curious	**intelligent**	outspoken	traditional
exciting	lonely	part-time	unique
friendly			

Example

f. He is a very *intelligent* person. He learns very quickly and he knows a lot of things.

27. She felt very _____ when her husband was away on a business trip.

28. Foreign students sometimes feel _____ and miss their countries and families.

29. We felt very _____ about the new city and wanted to know many things about it.

30. He's a very unhappy person. He always looks _____.

31. He works only a few hours a day because he has a _____ job.

32. Famous actors and actresses are often very _____. The men are handsome and the women are beautiful.

33. She works very hard because she wants to be _____ in her career.

34. Our vacation was very _____. We didn't feel bored for a moment.

35. They are a very _____ family. They like to follow the old customs of their country.

36. He is a very special and _____ person. There is no one else like him.

37. An _____ person is not afraid to express his real opinions even if they offend other people.

38. Cats and mice are not usually _____ to each other.

Now supply the appropriate preposition. You may use the same word more than one time.

about	at	from	of
among	for	in	**to**

Example
g. Yukio wanted to return __*to*__ Japan.

39. Cindy wanted to live _____ New York.

40. He left _____ work in the afternoon.

41. I met my friend _____ school _____ 10:00 _____ the morning.

42. He usually goes to sleep _____ 11:00 _____ night.

43. She received a letter _____ her boyfriend.

44. The child was afraid _____ the dark.

45. The class meets _____ 11:00 a.m. _____ 1:00 p.m.

Dictation/Cloze

Listen as your teacher reads, and write the words that you hear in the blanks:

Yukio's company _____ him to work _____ its New
                        1   2
York City office for half a year. This _____ Yukio's first experience
                                              3
living in the United States. Yukio _____ very sad and lonely until
                                          4

he _____ Cindy. Cindy _____ a new clerk who

        5   6

_____ to work _____ Yukio's office part-time. Yukio and

    7   8

Cindy _____ very well together. They _____ about many

        9   10

things. Cindy _____ Yukio her dreams of having a _____

           11   12

business _____. She _____ that she _____ really

        13   14   15

interested in getting married or _____ children. She

                         16

just _____ to _____ her _____. Yukio

      17   18   19

_____ Cindy _____ very different from the other women

    20   21

he _____. Similarly, Cindy _____ Yukio _____

      22   23   24

among the men she _____. Soon the two _____ in love.

              25   26

    But now they have a problem. Yukio wants _____ marry

                   27

Cindy and live _____ Japan _____ her. Cindy

          28   29

_____ to stay in New York and _____ her _____.

    30   31   32

What _____ you _____ Yukio and Cindy _____

        33   34   35

_____?

    36

Reading Comprehension

Circle the letter of the correct answers to the following questions:

   1. The main idea of this reading passage is:
      a. A man misses his country.
      b. American people and Japanese people cannot understand each other.
      c. There can be difficulties in falling in love with a person from another culture.
      d. Businessmen and their clerks often have romances.

2. A detail of this reading passage is:
   a. Cindy didn't want to be a traditional wife, but wanted to pursue a business career instead.
   b. Cindy was a part-time clerk who dreamed of working in Japan.
   c. Yukio lived in New York City for eight months.
   d. Yukio and Cindy worked in the same office for years.

3. According to the reading passage, which of the following sentences is true?
   a. Cindy didn't like Japan.
   b. Cindy was a student and a businesswoman.
   c. Yukio was a student and a businessman.
   d. Cindy was a student and a clerk.

4. According to the reading passage, which of the following sentences is *not* true?
   a. Cindy wanted a successful business career.
   b. Cindy didn't want to be a traditional wife and mother.
   c. Yukio didn't want to stay in New York.
   d. Yukio and Cindy didn't get along well when they first met.

5. In your opinion, based on the reading passage, which of the following sentences is true?
   a. Yukio thought people in New York were the same as people in Japan.
   b. Cindy had many other Japanese boyfriends before Yukio.
   c. Cindy was Yukio's first American girlfriend.
   d. Yukio spoke very little English.

6. Which pair has the words that are most similar in meaning?
   a. *career* and *study*
   b. *confused* and *miserable*
   c. *clerk* and *student*
   d. *get along* and *have a good relationship*

Guessing Meanings from Context

Guess the meanings of the italicized words from the context. Circle the letter of the word or words that are most similar in meaning to the italicized word(s):

Example

People sometimes *find* New York City strange and difficult.
   a. opposite of "lose"
   b. hard
   c. look for
   d. have the opinion; consider

1. It's often difficult for people to *get accustomed* to life in a new place.
   a. be customers
   b. get used to; adjust to
   c. get dressed
   d. go to sleep

2. He missed his family and *longed* to see them again.
   a. wrote
   b. wanted very much
   c. opposite of "short"
   d. tall

3. His parents *didn't get along.* They fought all the time.
   a. had a bad relationship
   b. had a good relationship
   c. get out
   d. agreed

4. Cindy wanted to work hard and *get ahead* in her career.
   a. advance and be successful
   b. stop working
   c. go out
   d. profession

5. He is a very *nosy* person! He asks everyone very personal questions about their lives.
   a. nice
   b. sick
   c. too curious
   d. ears

6. All the students feel very happy and excited when vacation time *draws near.*
   a. finishes
   b. pictures
   c. approaches
   d. take pictures

7. The weather was beautiful. There was warm *sunshine* and not a cloud in the sky.
   a. light from the sun
   b. beach
   c. nice day
   d. summer

8. The grandmother always smiled when she saw her grandson. He brought a lot of *sunshine* into her life.
   a. sunlight
   b. nice day
   c. happiness
   d. laugh

Words with Multiple Meanings

The word *get* can have different meanings, depending on the context in which it is used. Below are just a few of the possible meanings of the word *get:*

become	come	obtain	respond to (answer, attend to)
bring	go	receive	understand

Choose from the words above to identify the meaning of the word *get* in the following sentences. You can use the same word more than one time.

Example

It was difficult for Yukio to *get* accustomed to life in New York.

become

1. I always *get* presents for my birthday. _____

2. *"Get* in the house right now," said the mother to her child. "You're late for dinner." _____

3. Why do we spell the word *know* with a *k* if we don't pronounce *k*? I don't *get* it. _____

4. "I want you to leave my house right now," she said in an angry voice. *"Get* out!" _____

5. *"Get* me a cup of coffee and a piece of cake, please," the customer said to the waiter. _____

6. He *gets* tired when he works all day. _____

7. Please *get* the telephone! It's ringing and ringing! _____

8. Please *get* the door! Someone is knocking! _____

Group Activities

SMALL GROUP RETELLING OF STORY AND DISCUSSION

Work with a small group of students. Each student in the group can tell a little of the story of Yukio and Cindy until the entire story has been retold. After that, each student can give his or her opinion of the story. Should Yukio and Cindy get married? Should they separate? Should they live in New York or Japan or another place? One student in the group can write the opinions of the other students and later report them to the class.

ROLE-PLAYS

Divide the class into small groups or pairs. Each group or pair can choose one of the following situations to role-play for the rest of the class:

1. Yukio and Cindy are having a conversation about their situation. Write a dialogue for Yukio and Cindy to role-play for the rest of the class.

2. Imagine that Cindy tells her parents that she is marrying Yukio and going to live in Japan. Write a dialogue for Cindy and her parents to role-play for the rest of the class.

3. Imagine that Yukio tells his parents that he is staying in New York and marrying Cindy. Write a dialogue for Yukio and his family to role-play for the rest of the class.

4. Imagine another situation where two people from different countries meet and fall in love. Write a dialogue for the two people to role-play for the rest of the class.

5. Did you or someone you know ever have the experience of falling in love with a person from another country? If so, tell the rest of the class about this. After you finish telling the story, the rest of the class can write it.

CLASS DEBATE

Divide the class into two teams. One team can write all the reasons why Yukio and Cindy should stay together. The other team can write all the reasons why Yukio and Cindy should separate. Then, each team can present its reasons. Each team must answer the arguments of the other team.

Serial Marriages

Marriage is still a popular institution in the United States, but divorce is becoming almost as "popular." Most American people get married, but, at the present time, fifty per cent[a] of American marriages end in divorce. However, four out of five[b] divorced people do not stay single. They get married a second time to new partners.[c] Sociologists[d] tell us that in the next century, most American people will marry three or four times in one life-time. Alvin Toffler, an American sociologist, calls this new social form *serial*[e] *marriages*. In his book *Future Shock*, Toffler gives many reasons for this change in American marriage. In modern society, people's lives don't stay the same for very long. Americans frequently change their jobs, their homes, and their circles of friends. So, the person who was a good husband or wife ten years ago is sometimes not as good ten years later. After some years of marriage, a husband and wife can feel that their lives have become very different, and they don't share the same interests any more. For this reason, Toffler says, people in the twenty-first century will not plan to marry only one person for an entire*ᶠ* lifetime. They will plan to stay married to one person for perhaps five or ten years, and then marry another. Most Americans will expect to have a "marriage career" that includes three or four marriages.

Skim the above reading and write the main idea in one or two sentences. You can work alone or with a partner:

_____

_____

_____

Now scan the reading for the following information:

1. At the present time, do many American people get married?

   _____

2. What percentage (%) of American people get divorced?

   _____

3. What percentage of divorced Americans remarry (marry again)?

   _____

4. What do sociologists say?

   _____

5. Who is Alvin Toffler? What name does he give to this new form of marriage?

   _____

6. Why do people in modern society frequently get divorced and remarried?

   _____

7. According to Toffler, what will most people's idea of marriage be in the twenty-first century?

   _____

*ª*50% *ᵇ*4/5 *ᶜ*husbands or wives; one of a couple *ᵈ*social scientists; scientists who study society *ᵉ*one after another; consecutive *ᶠ*complete, whole

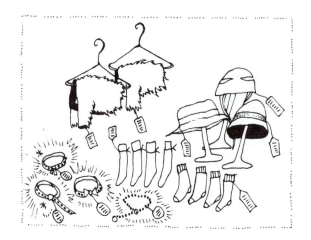

chapter 6

Rich Pets, Poor Pets

There Is, There Are

Pre-reading Questions

In your country, is it usual for people to have dogs, cats, or other types of animals in their homes?

How do people treat these animals (or *pets*)? Do they buy special food for them? Do they buy special clothing for them?

Look at the pictures and tell what you see.

Rich Pets, Poor Pets

There are different ideas about pets in different parts of the world.[1] In most cultures, animals have an inferior position to human beings.[2] In some instances, however, people treat their pets like members of their families, or perhaps better.[3] In the United States and Europe, where pets are very popular, there are special shops that sell jewelry, clothing, and gourmet food for cats and dogs.[4] There are shops on fashionable streets in New York City, for example, that sell gold and diamond collars, fur jackets, hats and mittens for pets.[5]

In many countries of the world, there is special food for pets.[6] It is common for supermarkets in many places to sell cat food and dog food.[7] However, in Nice, France, there is a special restaurant for dogs. Dogs are the only customers.[8] There is seating for twenty of them.[9] On the menu, there is a variety of special gourmet dishes for the dogs to choose from. There is a sausage dish, a turkey dish, and a pasta dish, among others. For dessert, there is an assortment of French cheeses and, of course, dog biscuits.[10]

In the United States, there is a very rich cat who can afford to go to any restaurant he chooses. His name is Kitty Cat.[11] Kitty Cat inherited one hundred thousand dollars when his owner died. In addition, the owner left Kitty Cat a beautiful mansion to live in.[12] There is a person who comes to the mansion every day to feed and take care of Kitty Cat.[13]

Of course, in most parts of the world, pets don't live in such wealth and luxury.[14] There is a more practical and functional attitude toward pets.[15] People own cats and dogs because they keep away mice and other unwanted animals.[16] Certainly, owners generally have some affectionate feelings for their pets. However, they do not see them as equal to family members.[17] In most places in the world, there isn't any special clothing, or jewelry, or gourmet food for animals. There aren't any special restaurants for dogs. There are no rich cats who live in mansions.[18]

Pets around the world live in a great variety of ways, just as people do.[19]

1. Are there the same ideas about pets in every part of the world?
2. What is true in most cultures?
3. What is true in some instances?
4. What kinds of shops are there in the United States and Europe?
5. What kinds of things do shops on fashionable streets in New York City sell for pets?
6. What is there in many countries of the world?
7. What is it common for supermarkets in many places to sell?
8. What kind of restaurant is there in Nice, France?
9. How many dogs is there seating for?
10. What is on the menu in this restaurant?

11. Who is Kitty Cat?
12. Why is Kitty Cat rich? Where does Kitty Cat live?
13. Who feeds and takes care of Kitty Cat?
14. Do pets in all parts of the world live in wealth and luxury?
15. What kind of attitude is there toward pets in most parts of the world?
16. Why do some people own pets?
17. How do these owners feel about their pets?
18. Is there any special clothing, jewelry, restaurants, or mansions for these animals?
19. Do pets and people around the world all live in the same way?

There Is, There Are

We use *there is* and *there are* to tell about the existence of certain objects, people, places, or other nouns.

When we tell about the existence of a singular noun(s), we use *there is*:

there is	singular noun
There is	a cat.
There is	a cat, a dog, and a bird.

When we tell about the existence of a plural noun, we use *there are*:

there are	plural noun
There are	three cats.

To form a question, we reverse the position of *there* and *is*, or *there* and *are*:

is/ *are*	*there*	singular noun(s)/ plural noun
Is	there	a cat?
Is	there	a cat, a dog, and a bird?
Are	there	three cats?

To form the negative, we put *not* after the verb *to be*:

there	*is/* *are*	*not*	singular noun(s)/ plural noun
There	is	not	a cat.
There	is	not	a cat, a dog, and a bird.
There	are	not	three cats.

It is usual to form the following contractions with *there is* and *there are*:

there + is = *there's*
there + are = *there're* (common in spoken rather than written
    English)
there + is + not = *there's not* or
                            there isn't
there + are + not = *there're not* or
                            there aren't

The past tense of *there is* is *there was*. The past tense of *there are* is *there were*. These past tense forms are *not* contracted. However, the negative forms are contracted in this way: *there wasn't* or *there weren't*.

Vocabulary

Write the appropriate verbs in the spaces provided. Do not use the same verb more than one time. Write the correct tense of the verb that is needed:

afford	feed	leave	take care
choose	inherit	protect	treat
die	keep away	**sell**	

Example

   a. Supermarkets in many countries __*sell*__ dog and cat

   food which customers buy for their pets.

1. At the restaurant for dogs in France, the dog customers can
   _____ from a variety of dinners and desserts on the menu.

2. No animal or plant lives forever. Every living thing _____
   eventually.

3. The children _____ a lot of money when their rich uncle
   died. He _____ them a fortune.

4. We _____ our cat whenever he is hungry.

5. _____ from that hot stove! You can hurt yourself if you go
   near it.

6. Very rich people can ＿＿＿＿＿＿＿ to buy diamond collars and fur jackets for their dogs, but poor people can't.

7. We ＿＿＿＿＿＿＿ of our plants. We always give them enough water and sunlight.

8. Umbrellas and raincoats ＿＿＿＿＿＿＿ us from the rain.

9. That company ＿＿＿＿＿＿＿ its workers very well. They receive good salaries, vacations, and benefits.

Now supply the appropriate noun. Do not use the same word more than one time.

assortment	customer	mansion	**pet**
attitude	dessert	member	position
biscuit	dish	mice (mouse)	sausage
cheese	human being	mittens	seating
clothing	jewelry	owner	turkey
collar	luxury	pasta	variety

Example

b. Cats and dogs are very popular _**pets**_ in the United States.

10. Americans often eat ＿＿＿＿＿＿＿ for dinner on Thanksgiving.

11. He worked very hard because he wanted to get a high ＿＿＿＿＿＿＿ in his company.

12. There is always ＿＿＿＿＿＿＿ on the menu in Italian restaurants.

13. The theater holds 500 people. There is ＿＿＿＿＿＿＿ for 475 and standing room for 25.

14. My favorite Italian ＿＿＿＿＿＿＿ is pasta with vegetables.

15. In my English class, there are students from a ＿＿＿＿＿＿＿ of countries.

16. This is a very popular restaurant. There are always so many ＿＿＿＿＿＿＿ eating here.

17. The _____ of a popular restaurant probably makes a lot of money.

18. Americans often eat cake or ice cream for _____. In other countries, fruit or cheese is more usual.

19. Countries vary in their _____ toward public affection. The customs of some countries permit it, but others don't.

20. She always wears earrings, rings, and bracelets. She loves _____.

21. For dessert, there is an _____ of fruit: apples, bananas, melons, grapes, and others.

22. _____ is made from milk and is popular in European countries like France and Switzerland.

23. She put on her _____ because her hands were cold.

24. In the summer, people don't wear heavy _____ because the weather is warm.

25. _____ are the most intelligent of all the animals.

26. The sweater has a high _____ that covers his neck.

27. The rich family lives in a big _____ that has twenty-five rooms.

28. A Mercedes-Benz car is a _____ that most people can't afford.

29. He likes many different kinds of meat, but especially _____ because it is so spicy.

30. Four _____ of our class speak Spanish.

Now supply the appropriate adjective. Use each word only one time.

beautiful	functional	popular
expensive	fur	practical
fashionable	gourmet	**rich**

Example

c. *Rich* _____ people have a lot of money.

31. Jewelry is often made from _____ metals like silver and gold.

32. _____ coats are very expensive, very beautiful, and also very warm in the winter.

33. A diamond is a very _____ and expensive white stone.

34. A _____ person is the opposite of a dreamer.

35. Caviar and pate are examples of _____ foods.

36. A watch is a fine gift because it is both attractive and _____. It can be beautiful to look at and useful to have.

37. Elegant women in cities like New York, Paris, and Rome often wear very _____ clothing.

38. Many Americans like pizza. It is a very _____ food in the United States.

Now supply the appropriate preposition. You may use the same word more than one time.

about   for   from   **in**   of   on   to   toward

Example

d. The restaurant for dogs is _*in*_ France.

39. There are many lovely shops _____ that street.

40. The class meets _____ 9:00 _____ 11:00 A.M.

41. He comes _____ class every day.

42. In this chapter, we read an article _____ pets.

43. In many parts _____ the world, people own pets.

44. The rich man bought a diamond collar _____ his dog.

45. She has a good attitude _____ her job. She works hard and she enjoys it.

46. We studied our lesson _____ two hours.

47. If you look _____ the west, you can see the sunset.

Reading Comprehension

Circle the letter of the correct answers to the following questions:

1. The main idea of this reading passage is:
   a. Dogs enjoy fine restaurants.
   b. A rich cat can afford to go to any restaurant.
   c. People treat pets in very different ways in different parts of the world.
   d. It's stupid to have special food, clothing, and jewelry for animals.

2. A detail of this reading passage is:
   a. Cheese is a good dessert for a dog.
   b. In some parts of the world, there is special food, clothing, and jewelry for dogs.
   c. Some people spend too much money on their pets.
   d. New York City has a lot of fashionable shops.

3. According to the reading passage, which of the following sentences is true?
   a. There are many owners of dogs and cats in the United States and Europe.
   b. There are restaurants for dogs in every city in France.
   c. Kitty Cat inherited several million dollars.
   d. Dogs and cats never wear clothing.

4. According to the reading passage, which of the following sentences is *not* true?
   a. Kitty Cat is a very rich cat.
   b. Some shops in New York City sell automobiles for pets.
   c. The restaurant in Nice has seating for twenty dogs.
   d. In some parts of the world, there is a more practical, functional attitude toward pets.

5. Which pair has the words that are most similar in meaning?
   a. *pet* and *dog*
   b. *assortment* and *variety*
   c. *sausage* and *diamond*
   d. *diamonds* and *jewelry*

6. In your opinion, which of the following sentences is probably true?
  a. Dogs and cats like to wear expensive furs and jewelry.
  b. Many poor people visit Nice, France.
  c. People in every part of the world like to buy diamonds and furs for their pets.
  d. In some instances, animals have better food and clothing than some people do.

Guessing Meanings from Context

Guess the meanings of the italicized words from the context. Circle the letter of the word or words that are most similar in meaning to the italicized word(s):

> **Example**
>
> In a few *instances*, pets wear furs and diamonds and eat expensive food, but in most *instances*, they don't.
> **a.** shops
> **(b.)** cases
> **c.** time
> **d.** minutes

1. Kitty Cat can afford to buy many things because he is a very *wealthy* cat.
  a. poor
  b. happy
  c. big
  d. rich

2. Cats and dogs usually need people to feed and *look after* them.
  a. see
  b. wash
  c. give food to them
  d. take care of

3. Kitty Cat's owner left his pet one hundred thousand dollars in his *will*. Did he also leave money to his family?
  a. future
  b. document that tells who will receive a person's money after he dies
  c. a paper that tells information about a person's pet
  d. wallet

4. He cooks and eats only the very best foods. He is a real *gourmet*.
   a. person who likes to eat everything
   b. person who likes to eat foods from different countries
   c. person who knows a lot about food and likes it very much
   d. person who eats too much

5. There are so many delicious desserts on the menu that it's difficult to *pick out* just one.
   a. pie
   b. fruit
   c. choose
   d. change

6. Wealthy people often stay at beautiful, *luxurious* hotels when they travel.
   a. expensive and elegant
   b. old
   c. a lot of money
   d. lucky

7. In cities like New York, Paris, and Rome, women and men often wear very *stylish* clothes.
   a. ugly
   b. poor
   c. fashionable
   d. sell

8. People in England like to have tea and *biscuits* in the afternoon.
   a. cookies
   b. dogs
   c. dog food
   d. breakfast

9. In most cultures, human beings have a *superior* position to animals.
   a. inferior
   b. successful
   c. persons
   d. higher

Structure Practice

When forming the negative of *there is* or *there are*, we often say, "there isn't/aren't *any*" + noun(s). Or we may say, "there is/are *no* + noun(s).

Listen as your teacher reads the following sentences. The sentences contain false information. Make the sentences negative to make them true.

Example

There are elephants in our classroom.

There aren't any elephants in our classroom.

There are no elephants in our classroom.

1. In New York City, there are shops that sell motorcycles for dogs.

   _____

2. There is wine on the menu at the restaurant for dogs in Nice, France.

   _____

3. In South America, there are restaurants for giraffes.

   _____

4. In the United States, there are shops that sell cigars and cigarettes for cats.

   _____

5. There is a hotel for monkeys in Paris.

   _____

6. There are mice in this room!

   _____

Dictation/Cloze

Listen as your teacher reads, and write the words that you hear in the blank spaces.

_____ _____ many different _____ about
     1   2   3

_____ in different parts _____ the world. In most places,
   4   5

_____ _____ a practical _____ toward pets.
   6   7   8

Pets have an inferior position to _____ _____. In some
                        9   10

countries, _____, some pets live more _____ lives than
         11   12

many people do. In the United States, _____ _____ a

                                                     13   14

_____ who lives in a mansion. This cat _____ one hun-

    15   16

dred _____ dollars when his owner _____.

        17   18

    In some American cities, _____ _____ _____

                                     19   20   21

who buy jewelry, _____, and gourmet _____ for their pets.

                    22   23

Many countries sell pet food in _____, but in France, _____

                                     24   25

_____ _____ special _____ for dogs. Dogs are

    26   27   28

the only _____. _____ _____ delicious

             29   30   31

_____ _____ on the menu. For example, _____

    32   33   34

_____ _____ turkey _____, _____

    35   36   37   38

_____ dish, and _____ pasta _____.

    39   40   41

    In different parts _____ the world, _____

                                42   43

_____ different _____ of life for both _____ and their

    44   45   46

_____.

    47

Group Activities

SMALL GROUP DISCUSSION

Work with a small group of students and discuss the following questions: Are there restaurants for dogs in your country? Are there special shops that sell clothing, jewelry, and gourmet foods for dogs? What is your opinion of these things? What attitude do people in your country have toward animals? In your opinion, should people treat animals like family members? Should people leave money to animals in their wills? One student can write the opinions of the members of the group and later report them to the rest of the class.

ROLE-PLAY

Work in pairs. Choose one of the following situations to role-play for the rest of the class:

1. Write a dialogue between the owner of the restaurant for dogs and a newspaper reporter. The reporter wants to know why the owner decided to open a restaurant for dogs. The owner explains his reasons. Perform the dialogue for the rest of the class.

2. Write a dialogue between Kitty Cat's owner and his lawyer. The owner explains to the lawyer why he wants to leave all his money to his cat. Perform the dialogue.

3. Write a dialogue between two people who have different attitudes toward pets. One person says he wishes to buy a fur coat and diamond collar for his pet's birthday. The other person finds this ridiculous. Perform the dialogue for the class.

SIMON SAYS

Listen as your teacher tells you to act out the various actions mentioned in this chapter and previous chapters. Act out the actions only if your teacher first says the words *Simon says*. If you make a mistake, you must stop playing the game. The last person left standing is the winner.

Possible commands are:

Put on a hat.
Put on some mittens.
Put on a beautiful fur coat.

Put on a diamond necklace.
Feed some pigeons (birds).

OTHER ACTIVITIES FOR DISCUSSION AND WRITING

1. An Australian philosopher named Peter Singer wrote a book called *Animal Liberation*. In this book, Singer says that animals should have the same right to life that human beings do. He doesn't believe that human beings should kill other animals for food and clothing. He doesn't think that human beings have the right to exploit other animals just because human beings have superior intelligence.

What do you think of Peter Singer's ideas? Do you agree or disagree?

2. Do you have a pet? Write a short paragraph describing your pet. What kind of pet is it? How big is it? What color is it? How does it behave? What kind of personality does it have?

Famous Vegetarians

People in most parts of the world eat meat. However, in many cultures throughout history, some people have thought it wrong to use animals for food. These people abstained[a] from eating meat. Persons who do not eat meat are called *vegetarians*.

Some of the world's most famous philosophers and artists were vegetarians. Buddha, the great Indian philosopher and mystic, did not eat meat. He believed that abstaining from meat could help a person's spiritual life. Also, Plato, the great Greek philosopher, thought that human beings[b] should not eat other animals, but rather[c] use plants for their food.

Like Plato, the nineteenth century English poet Percy Bysshe Shelley believed it was very cruel[d] for persons to kill animals for food. Shelley believed that human beings should eat a simple diet of fruits, nuts, and vegetables. In one of his poems*, he wrote:

Never again may blood of bird or beast[e]
Stain[f] with its venomous[g] stream[h]
A human feast![i]

When the English playwright[j] George Bernard Shaw read Shelley's writings, he too became a vegetarian. Shaw lived a very active life until the age of 94 on his meatless diet.

The eighteenth century French writer-philosophers Voltaire and Rousseau also advocated[k] a vegetarian diet, as did the English political philosopher Jeremy Bentham. As in the present time, many people in Bentham's time believed that it was *not* wrong to kill animals because animals could not think or reason. In answer to these people, Bentham said: "The question is not 'Can they reason?' nor 'Can they talk?' but 'Can they suffer[l]?'"

A great American writer of the twentieth century, Isaac Bashevis Singer, expressed his vegetarian beliefs this way. When someone asked him if he was a vegetarian for health reasons, Singer answered, "Not for my health, but for the health of the chickens."

Skim the above reading and write the main idea in one or two sentences:

_____

_____

[a]stayed away from, avoided [b]people [c]instead [d]opposite of 'kind,' and 'good' [e]animal [f]soil (make dirty) [g]poisonous [h]flow [i]meal [j]writer of plays for the theater [k]believed in and recommended [l]feel pain

*"The Revolt of Islam," by Percy Bysshe Shelley.

Now scan the reading for the following information:

1. Why are some people vegetarians?

    _____

2. Who was Buddha? Why was he a vegetarian?

    _____

3. Name a great Greek philosopher who was a vegetarian.

    _____

4. What did the poet Shelley believe? What idea did he express in one of his poems?

    _____

5. What English playwright was a vegetarian? Why did he become a vegetarian? How old was he when he died?

    _____

6. Name two French writer-philosophers who were vegetarians. In what century did they live?

    _____

7. Who was Jeremy Bentham? When did he live?

    _____

8. Why do some people believe it is *not* wrong to kill animals? What answer did Bentham give to these people?

    _____

9. Who is Isaac Bashevis Singer? How did he express his vegetarian beliefs?

    _____

chapter 7

The Amazing Story of the Palm Leaf Libraries

Review of Tenses: Simple Present, Present Continuous, Simple Past; Introduction of Will

Pre-reading Questions

Look at the picture. Tell what you see. What country do you think it is?

What is a fortune-teller? Did you ever go to a fortune-teller? Did this person tell you about your past, present, and future?

Do you think it is possible for one person to know another person's future?

The Amazing Story of the Palm Leaf Libraries

A German author named Johannes von Buttlar tells an amazing story in his best-selling book called *Time-Slip*.[1] Von Buttlar writes that in India, there are special, mysterious libraries.[2] These libraries don't have books. Instead, they have very large palm leaves which are hundreds of years old.[3] The life story of one person is written on each palm leaf.[4] The palm leaf tells the story of the person's past, present, and future.[5] Wise men wrote the stories on these palm leaves centuries ago.[6] However, the truly amazing thing is that, if any person living today visits one of the palm leaf libraries, this person will find a palm leaf with his or her own life story. The palm leaf will tell this person's past, present, and future.[7] Perhaps you are wondering how it is possible for wise men who lived centuries ago to know the lives of people living today. Von Buttlar explains that these wise men had the power to know the future. With this power, the wise men could foresee the events in the lives of people who would be born centuries after them.[8] The wise men could also foresee which of these people would go to the palm leaf libraries, and so wrote palm leaves only for these persons.[9]

1. Who is Johannes von Buttlar?
2. What does von Buttlar write in his book *Time-Slip*?
3. Do the mysterious libraries have books?
4. What is written on each palm leaf?
5. What story does the palm leaf tell?
6. Who wrote the stories on the palm leaves?
7. What will happen if a person living today visits one of the palm leaf libraries?
8. How is it possible for men who lived centuries ago to know the lives of people living today?
9. Did the wise men write palm leaves for every person in the world?
10. What do you think of this amazing story?

Introducing Will

We use *will* before the base form of a verb to describe a future action:

subject	*will*	infinitive verb
I (you, he, she, it, we, they)	will	go.

To form a question, we reverse the position of the subject and *will*:

will	subject	infinitive verb
Will	I (you, he, she, it, we, they)	go?

To form a negative sentence, we put the word *not* after the word *will*:

subject	*will*	*not*	infinitive verb
I (you, he, she, it, we, they)	will	not	go.

Often, we put *will* and *not* together to form the following contraction:

will + not = won't

PRACTICE WITH *WILL*

Listen as your teacher reads the following sentences about your future. If you don't agree with the information in the sentence, make it negative.

Example

[teacher reads] You will go to India and visit a palm leaf library one year from now.

[student responds] *I won't go to India and visit a palm leaf library one year from now.*

1. You will make ten million dollars one year from now.

   _____

2. You will marry a famous movie star one year from today.

   _____

3. You will have ten children ten years from now.

   _____

4. You will speak perfect English six weeks from now.

   _____

5. You will own an airplane one year from now.

   _____

6. You will fly in a spaceship with some spacemen tonight.

    _____

7. You will have dinner with the President of the United States at the White House next week.

    _____

8. You will dance at a disco with a famous rock-and-roll singer next weekend.

    _____

Vocabulary

Write the appropriate verbs in the spaces provided. Do not use the same verb more than one time. Be sure to use the appropriate verb tense. You may use the word *will* to describe a future action.

be born	**find**	know	wonder
can	foresee	live	**write**
explain	have	**tell**	

Examples

a. Wise men ___*wrote*___ the life stories of persons on palm leaves centuries ago.

b. The palm leaves ___*tell*___ the story of a person's past, present, and future.

c. If persons living today go to the palm leaf libraries, they ___*will find*___ palm leaves with their own life stories.

1. Sometimes I _____ if it really is possible to see the future.

2. Last summer, he _____ the opportunity to visit India.

3. Did I pass the examination? I _____ my grade tomorrow.

4. I don't understand this grammar. _____you _____ it to me?

5. When I was in my country, I _____ speak my native language all the time.

6. In July and August, they _____ in their summer house.

7. Their son _____ on July 16, 1984.

8. Some people believe that fortune tellers can _____ the future.

Now supply the appropriate noun. Do not use the same word more than one time.

author   event   palm leaf   person
century   **library**   people   power

> **Example**
> d. Students often go to the *library* to study and to borrow books.

9. The American _____ Ernest Hemingway wrote many novels and stories.

10. The year 1879 was in the nineteenth _____.

11. Many _____ live and work in a big city.

12. There is a _____ in my class who speaks four languages.

13. New jobs, marriage, and the birth of children are important _____ in people's lives.

14. _____ grow on palm trees.

15. This car has the _____ to go 150 miles per hour.

Now supply the appropriate adjective.

amazing   best-selling   mysterious   **special**   wise

> **Example**
> e. A palm leaf library is not just an ordinary library. It is quite a *special* library.

16. She had an ＿＿＿＿＿＿＿ power to foresee the future of every person she met. Her ability was incredible.

17. Socrates and Confucius understood many things about life. They were very ＿＿＿＿＿＿＿ men.

18. That novel sold more than one hundred thousand copies. It was a ＿＿＿＿＿＿＿ book last year.

19. Nobody really understands how the Egyptians built the pyramids. It's very ＿＿＿＿＿＿＿.

Now supply the appropriate preposition. You may use the same word more than one time.

> in   of   on   **to**   with
>
> **Example**
> f. He went ＿*to*＿ India last summer.

20. One ＿＿＿＿ the people in the class is from France.

21. He is writing ＿＿＿＿ a piece of paper.

22. She is writing ＿＿＿＿ her notebook.

23. He writes ＿＿＿＿ his left hand.

24. ＿＿＿＿ his great ability in business, he can make a lot ＿＿＿＿ money.

25. Which ＿＿＿＿ the students is from Japan?

Now supply the appropriate adverb. You may use each word more than one time.

> however   instead   **only**
>
> **Example**
> g. He lives ＿*only*＿ two blocks from the university.

26. She wants tea ＿＿＿＿ of coffee.

27. Don't let the children read those magazines! They are ＿＿＿＿ for adults.

28. He likes New York City. _____, he doesn't like the noise and pollution.

29. Can we see a play _____ of a movie tonight?

Dictation/Cloze

Listen as your teacher reads, and write the words that you hear in the blank spaces.

Johannes von Buttlar _____ an _____ story in his

　　　　　　　　　　　　　　1　　　　　　　2

_____ book *Time-Slip*. In this book, the _____ writes

　　3　　　　　　　　　　　　　　　　　　　4

about the _____ palm leaf _____ in India. In these

　　　　　　5　　　　　　　　　6

libraries, _____ _____ palm _____ _____

　　　　7　　　　　8　　　　　　　9　　　　　10

the life stories _____ various persons written _____

　　　　　　　11　　　　　　　　　　　　　　12

them. _____ men _____ the life stories _____

　　　13　　　　　　14　　　　　　　　　　　15

the palm leaves _____ ago. _____, if a person living

　　　　　　16　　　　　　17

today _____ one _____ these libraries, he or she

　　18　　　　　　　19

_____ _____ a palm leaf with his or her own life

　　20　　　　　　21

_____ on it. _____ you _____ _____

　22　　　　　　23　　　　　　24　　　　　25

how it is possible for wise men who _____ centuries ago to

　　　　　　　　　　　　　　　26

_____ the lives _____ men living today. Von Buttlar

　27　　　　　　　　28

_____ that the wise men _____ the _____

　29　　　　　　　　　　30　　　　　　31

to know the future. _____ this power, they _____

　　　　　　　　32　　　　　　　　　33

_____ which _____ would visit the libraries centuries

　34　　　　　35

later. The wise _____ _____ palm _____ only
             36   37   38

for these people. What _____ your _____ of von Buttlar's
                          39   40

_____ _____?
      41   42

Reading Comprehension

Circle the letter of the correct answers to the following questions:

1. The main idea of this reading passage is:
    a. *Time-Slip* was a best-selling book.
    b. A long time ago people had the power to know the future.
    c. People wrote on palm leaves before paper existed.
    d. In special libraries in India, there are mysterious centuries-old palm leaves that tell the life stories of people.

2. A detail of this reading passage is:
    a. If a person living today goes to one of these libraries, he or she will find a palm leaf with his or her own past, present, and future written on it.
    b. Johannes von Buttlar is American.
    c. Johannes von Buttlar is the author of the book *Time-Sleep.*
    d. If a person living today goes to a palm leaf library, a wise man will tell him his past, present, and future.

3. According to the reading passage, which of the following sentences is true?
    a. The palm leaf libraries contain the life stories of every person in the world.
    b. The palm leaf libraries contain the life stories of people who lived in the past.
    c. There is a palm leaf that tells the story of von Buttlar's life.
    d. The wise men who wrote the life stories on the palm leaves had the power to know the future.

4. According to the reading passage, which of the following sentences is *not* true?
    a. Wise men who lived hundreds of years ago wrote the life stories of people who are living today.
    b. There are many books in the palm leaf libraries.
    c. The wise men wrote palm leaves only for the people that would one day visit the palm leaf libraries.
    d. The palm leaf libraries are in India.

5. In your opinion, which of the following sentences is probably true?
   a. Von Buttlar wrote his book *Time-Slip* centuries ago.
   b. Von Buttlar has the power to foresee the future.
   c. Not many people were interested in von Buttlar's story.
   d. Many people were very interested in von Buttlar's story of the palm leaf libraries.

6. Which pair has the words that are most similar in meaning?
   a. *know* and *foresee*
   b. *amazing* and *special*
   c. *a century* and *a hundred years*
   d. *palm leaf* and *paper*

Guessing Meanings from Context

Guess the meanings of the italicized words from the context. Circle the letter of the word or words that are most similar in meaning to the italicized word(s):

> **Example**
>
> The story of the palm leaf libraries is really an *amazing* one.
> a. sad and depressing
> b. terrible
> c. incredible; very surprising
> d. funny

1. Each palm leaf has a *biography* of one person.
   a. picture
   b. education
   c. life story
   d. biology

2. The wise men had the power to *predict* the future of individuals.
   a. people
   b. problems
   c. foresee and tell
   d. psychic

3. Every night, the news announcer on television *forecasts* the weather for tomorrow.
   a. forgets
   b. knows for sure and tells the information
   c. nice day
   d. predicts, based on information he or she has

4. People who know the future have *psychic* powers.
   a. psychiatrist
   b. special physical abilities
   c. sick
   d. beyond the physical; supernatural

5. In many cultures, some people believe that *fortune-tellers* can give individuals personal information and advice about the future.
   a. rich people who like to talk about their money
   b. talkative people
   c. bankers
   d. persons that can tell about future events before they happen

6. Some fortune-tellers look at the *palm* of a person's hand to know his or her future.
   a. fingers
   b. the inside of the hand
   c. the outside of the hand
   d. the fingernails

7. Perhaps there really are people that are *capable* of knowing the future.
   a. have the ability
   b. crazy
   c. tell lies
   d. impossible

8. *Parapsychology* studies events that natural science and psychology cannot explain.
   a. an area of psychology that studies emotional problems
   b. psychiatry
   c. psychiatrists
   d. an area of study that explores psychic phenomena

Word Forms

WHAT IS A *PREFIX*?

A *prefix* is a group of letters we find at the beginning of a word. These letters have a specific meaning, and they modify or change the meaning of the rest of the word. For example, the letters *un-* are a prefix. *Un* means *not*. If we put these letters at the beginning of a word, they modify its meaning. *Un*happy means *not* happy. *Un*important means *not* important.

The letters *fore* are also a prefix. In many cases, *fore* means *before*. For example, the word *foresee* means to *see before*. So, if we say that a person can *foresee* events in the future, it means the person can *see* the events *before* they happen.

Sometimes, however, the prefix *fore* can also mean *in the front*. For example, the word *forearm* means the front of the arm, the part below the elbow, nearest to the hand.

Read the following sentences and decide if the prefix *fore* in the underlined words means *before* or *in the front*.

Examples

a. Every day, the announcer on the radio *forecasts* the weather for tomorrow. __*before*__

b. The *forehead* is above the eyebrows and below the hairline. __*in the front*__

1. Fortune-tellers believe they can *foretell* the future. _____

2. Pablo Picasso, the painter, is in the *forefront* of twentieth century art. _____

3. He bought the car on impulse, without much *forethought* of the finances. Now he is having difficulty paying for it. _____

4. Thomas Jefferson, Benjamin Franklin, and Aaron Burr were among the first Americans. They were the *forefathers* of Americans living today. _____

5. He made a lot of money because he had the *foresight* to invest in the growing company when it first began. _____

6. The *forefinger* is the first finger next to the thumb. _____

7. In the famous painting, the *Mona Lisa*, the woman with the mysterious smile is in the *foreground*. _____

8. We *forewarned* him of the heavy rainstorm, but he went out anyway. Now he is all wet! _____

Group Activities

SMALL GROUP DISCUSSION

Work with a small group of students and discuss the following topics. One student in the group can write the main points and opinions of all the students in the group, and later report these to the rest of the class:

1. What is your opinion of "The Amazing Story of the Palm Leaf Libraries"? Do you believe the story? Do you believe it is possible for some people to foresee the future? Is it possible for any person to know the events in the life of a person he has never met? Is it possible for a person to know the events in the life of a person who is not yet born?

2. Do people in your country sometimes talk to fortune-tellers when they have problems or want to know the future for some reason? Is it common for people to do this?

3. In your country, is there a tradition of palm-reading, face-reading, astrological forecasting, or other methods of knowing the future? Did you ever meet a person who told you about your future?

4. Did you ever have a dream about the future that later came true? Tell the other students about this dream.

ROLE-PLAYS

Choose one of the following situations to role-play for the rest of the class:

1. Are there any students in your class who can read palms, faces, or cards? If there are, ask these students to act the part of fortune-tellers and tell the past, present, or future of other students in the class. Remember to use *will* when you describe future events. For example, "You will make a lot of money," "You will have four children," etc.

2. Work in pairs. Imagine a dialogue between a fortune-teller and a customer. Write the dialogue and role-play it for the rest of the class.

3. Imagine that you go to a palm leaf library. You ask for the palm leaf with your life story. You read it. What does it say? What will happen to you in the future? How do you feel about what the palm leaf says? Are you happy? Surprised? Afraid? Excited?

LETTER-WRITING

Write a letter to yourself. In the letter, write all the things that you think will happen to you and to people close to you in one year. Where will you live one year from now? Will you study English? Will you have the same friends? Will you have a job? Will you have a new boyfriend or girlfriend? After you write your letter, put it into a stamped, self-addressed envelope, and give it to your teacher. Your teacher will mail the letter to you in one year, and you will see if you predicted your future correctly.

CLASS DEBATE

Divide the class into two teams. One team will write all the reasons why people should believe in fortune-tellers and other types of psychic phenomena. The other team will write all the reasons why people shouldn't believe these things. Then, each team will present its reasons to the class. Each team must be prepared to answer the points and arguments of the other team.

Edgar Cayce: An American Psychic

Some people believe that Edgar Cayce, an American man who lived in this century, had psychic powers. Cayce lived from 1877 to 1945 mostly in a small town in Virginia. He was not an educated man. As a child, he was a poor[a] student, and attended school only until the sixth grade (or until age 11).

When Cayce became a young man, he discovered he had the power to hypnotize himself. He could put himself into a very special mental state called a *trance*. While in this trance, he could answer many questions about people's lives and futures. He could tell sick people how to become well. Often he answered questions about people's health[b] that even doctors could not answer.

Cayce also answered questions about the future of the world. He correctly predicted when the first and second world wars would begin and end. He foresaw the Great Depression of 1929.

Today, in Edgar Cayce's town of Virginia Beach, there is a special organization called the *Association for Research and Enlightenment*. At this place, there are films and lectures[c] about Cayce's predictions and philosophy.[d] There is a bookstore and a library with all of his psychic "readings." If you are in the United States, you can visit the *Association* and learn more about this American psychic.

Skim the above reading and write the main idea in one or two sentences. You can work alone or with another student:

_____

_____

Now scan the reading for the following details:

1. When did Edgar Cayce live?

_____

2. Did he have a lot of education?

_____

3. What power did Cayce have?

_____

4. What world events did Cayce correctly predict?

_____

5. Where is the *Association for Research and Enlightenment*? What is this place?

_____

[a]not good   [b]physical state   [c]talks   [d]beliefs about life

chapter 8

Superstitions

The Present Real Conditional:
If . . . will

Pre-reading Questions

What is a superstition?

Look at the pictures. What superstitions do they show? Do you have these same superstitions in your country?

Superstitions

Every culture in the world believes certain superstitions.[1] Even societies that are very rational and scientific are sometimes a little bit superstitious.[2] For example, the United States is a country that is very advanced in science and technology. But even in American society, people sometimes believe superstitions. Americans consider "thirteen" an unlucky number. So, it is rare to find a building with a thirteenth floor in the United States.[3] There is always a twelfth and a fourteenth floor, but there is rarely a thirteenth floor. Many people believe that if you live or work on the thirteenth floor of a building, you will have bad luck.[4] Some people in the United States also believe that if Friday falls on the thirteenth day of the month, they will have bad luck.[5]

Some Americans believe they will have bad luck if they walk under a ladder.[6] Even if people say they are not superstitious, they will often avoid walking under a ladder.[7]

Often, people consider it unlucky to break a mirror. If a person breaks a mirror, he or she will have seven years of sad misfortune.[8]

Americans also think they will have bad luck if a black cat crosses their path.[9] A long time ago, people believed that black cats were really witches in disguise.[10] However, some things are thought to bring good luck. For example, some Americans believe if they carry a rabbit's foot, they will have good luck.[11] Other people believe they will have good luck if they find a four-leaf clover.[12] Others think they will have good luck if they find a penny on the ground and pick it up.[13]

Even if a society becomes very advanced in science and technology, its people will always remain a little bit superstitious.[14]

1. Which cultures believe superstitions?
2. Are societies that are rational and scientific also a little bit superstitious?
3. In the United States, do we often find buildings with thirteenth floors? Why not?
4. According to superstition, what will happen if you live or work on the thirteenth floor of a building?
5. According to superstition, what will happen if Friday falls on the thirteenth day of the month?
6. What do some Americans believe will happen if they walk under a ladder?
7. Will people who say they are not superstitious always walk under ladders?
8. According to superstition, what will happen if a person breaks a mirror?

9. What do Americans think will happen if a black cat crosses their path?
10. What did people believe a long time ago?
11. What do some Americans believe will bring them good luck?
12. What do other people believe?
13. What do others think?
14. Are all people in technologically advanced societies completely *un*superstitious?

The Present Real Conditional

We use the present real conditional to describe a real cause-and-effect situation; *if* the first condition is true, then the second *will* follow:

if	subject	present tense verb	object
If	you	break	a mirror

subject	*will*	infinitive verb	object
you	will	have	bad luck.

To make a question, we reverse *will* and the subject. The *if clause* stays the same:

will	subject	infinitive verb	object
Will	you	have	bad luck

if	subject	present tense verb	object
if	you	break	a mirror?

To make the *if clause* negative, we follow the rule for present tense negative; to make the *will clause* negative, we follow the rule for making *will* negative:

if	subject	form of *do*	*not*	infinitive verb	object
If	you	do (don't)	not	break	a mirror

subject	*will*	*not*	infinitive verb	object
you	will	not	have (won't)	bad luck.

PRACTICE WITH *IF . . . WILL*

Write about superstitions in your country using the *if . . . will* form:

Example

In Colombia, if Tuesday falls on the thirteenth day of the month, you will have bad luck.

1. _____
2. _____
3. _____
4. _____
5. _____

Vocabulary

Write the appropriate verbs in the spaces provided. Do not use the same verb more than one time:

avoid	break	cross	**have**
become	carry	fall	pick up
believe	consider	find	remain

Example

a. If you find a four-leaf clover, you will ___*have*___ good luck.

1. If you drop the mirror, it will _____ into a hundred pieces.
2. If the traffic light changes to green, we will _____ the street.
3. If you work too hard, you will _____ tired.

4. My birthday will ＿＿＿＿＿＿＿ on a Wednesday next year.

5. If you give us correct directions to the restaurant, we will ＿＿＿＿＿＿＿ it.

6. If he feels sick again tomorrow, he will ＿＿＿＿＿＿＿ in bed.

7. If you tell me the truth, I will ＿＿＿＿＿＿＿ you.

8. If you don't ＿＿＿＿＿＿＿ a lot of money in your wallet, you won't spend a lot of money when you go out.

9. If we take the train home early, we will ＿＿＿＿＿＿＿ the rush hour and crowds.

10. Please ＿＿＿＿＿＿＿ your clothes! Don't leave them on the floor!

11. Americans ＿＿＿＿＿＿＿ it lucky to carry a rabbit's foot.

Now supply the appropriate noun.

building	ground	misfortune	society
culture	ladder	path	superstition
disguise	**luck**	rabbit	technology
floor	mirror	science	witch
four-leaf clover			

Example

b. If you walk under a ladder, you will have bad
luck ＿＿＿＿＿.

12. Every country believes certain ＿＿＿＿＿＿＿. Some people accept them, and some people don't.

13. On Halloween in the United States, many people wear a ＿＿＿＿＿＿＿.

14. A ＿＿＿＿＿＿＿ is an ugly, old woman with a big black hat, a cat, and a broom. She also has magic powers.

15. A ＿＿＿＿＿＿＿ is an animal with white or black fur and very long ears.

16. There are many tall _____ in New York, including the World Trade Center's Twin Towers.

17. My apartment is on the third _____ of the building.

18. We had a picnic in the park. Everyone sat on the _____ and ate lunch.

19. While sitting on the grass, she found a _____! How lucky she was!

20. We rode our bicycles along a _____ in the woods.

21. In our English class, there are students from many different _____.

22. He climbed up on a _____ to paint the ceiling.

23. He lost all his money on his vacation! What a _____!

24. Physics, chemistry, and biology are all in the category of _____.

25. Computers, telephones, and medical machines are results of advanced _____.

26. She looked into the _____ and brushed her hair.

27. In American _____, there are people from many different ethnic groups and cultures.

Now supply the appropriate adjective.

advanced	rational	superstitious
lucky	sad	thirteen
rare	scientific	unlucky

Example
c. Americans think it is *lucky* to carry a rabbit's foot.

28. Many people think it is _____ to break a mirror.

29. It's very usual to find a three-leaf clover, but it's _____ to find a four-leaf clover.

30. The _____ person avoided walking under ladders or near black cats.

31. The _____ person always thought carefully before deciding anything. He never made emotional decisions.

32. The student was in the _____ class because he knew a lot of English grammar and vocabulary.

33. Electricity was an important _____ discovery that changed people's lives.

34. She feels very _____ and lonely because her best friend moved to another country.

35. He feels nervous because his birthday falls on Friday the _____ this year!

Now supply the appropriate preposition. You may use the same word more than one time.

    in   of   on   to   under

> **Example**
>
> d. Every culture *in* the world believes certain super-stitions.

36. If you break a mirror, you will have seven years _____ bad luck.

37. I found some money _____ the ground.

38. It's lucky _____ find a four-leaf clover.

39. His birthday is _____ the fourteenth _____ July.

40. We live _____ the twelfth floor _____ our apartment building.

41. You will be unlucky if you walk _____ a ladder.

42. When it rains, people walk _____ umbrellas.

Dictation/Cloze

Listen as your teacher reads, and write the words that you hear in the blank spaces.

Every country _____ the world _____ its own su-
1   2

perstitions. Even countries that are _____ in _____ and
3   4

_____ have their superstitions. In the United States, for example,
5

some people _____ that _____ you _____ under
6   7   8

a ladder, you _____ _____ bad luck. For this reason,
9   10

many people _____ walking _____ ladders.
11   12

People in many countries _____ that _____ a black
13   14

cat _____ your path, you _____ _____ bad luck.
15   16   17

A long time ago, people _____ that black cats _____
18   19

really witches in _____.
20

Of course, some actions bring good luck. Americans believe that

_____ you _____ a rabbit's foot, you _____
21   22   23

_____ good luck. You _____ also _____ good
24   25   26

luck _____ you _____ a penny _____ the
27   28   29

ground and _____ it _____. Many persons think you
30   31

_____ _____ lucky if you _____ a four-leaf
32   33   34

clover.

Even if a country _____ very _____ in science and
35   36

_____, people _____ always _____ a little bit
37   38   39

_____.
40

Reading Comprehension

Circle the letter of the correct answers to the following questions.

1. The main idea of this reading passage is:
   a. People should not be superstitious.
   b. People should try not to break mirrors.
   c. In the United States, nobody is superstitious.
   d. Even in scientifically advanced countries, some people are superstitious.

2. A detail of this reading passage is:
   a. Black cats are dangerous.
   b. Americans will have bad luck if they find a four-leaf clover.
   c. Some Americans believe they will have bad luck if they walk under a ladder.
   d. Rational people are never superstitious.

3. According to the reading passage, which of the following sentences is true?
   a. Nobody in the United States is superstitious.
   b. Some people believe they will have good luck if they eat a rabbit's foot.
   c. If a black cat crosses your path, you will have good luck.
   d. A long time ago, people thought that black cats were really witches.

4. According to the reading passage, which of the following sentences is *not* true?
   a. In the United States, it is not usual to find a building with a thirteenth floor.
   b. In the United States, it is usual to find buildings with thirteenth floors.
   c. Superstitions exist in many parts of the world.
   d. Even people who say they don't believe superstitions will often avoid walking under a ladder.

5. In your opinion, based on the reading passage, which of the following sentences is true?
   a. In societies that are advanced in science and technology, human beings are completely rational and scientific.
   b. People who believe superstitions are completely irrational and unscientific.
   c. Human beings are almost never completely rational and scientific.

    d. When societies become more advanced in science, there will be no more superstitions.

  6. Which pair has the words that are most similar in meaning?
    a. *floor* and *ground*
    b. *sad* and *bad*
    c. *ladder* and *staircase*
    d. *misfortune* and *bad luck*

Guessing Meanings from Context

Guess the meanings of the italicized words from the context. Circle the letter of the word or words that are most similar in meaning to the italicized word(s):

> **Example**
>
> The superstitious person *avoided* walking near black cats.
> **a.** enjoyed
> **b.** pet
> ⓒ kept away from
> **d.** approached carefully

  1. He saw a penny on the ground and *picked it up* with his hand.
    a. took it from the ground
    b. pushed it
    c. dropped it
    d. chose it

  2. After the child finished his class at school, his mother *picked him up* in her car.
    a. drove
    b. walked
    c. came to get him
    d. lifted him up

  3. Before the child started class in the morning, his mother drove him to school and *dropped him off.*
    a. picked him up in the car
    b. let him out of the car
    c. took him into the car
    d. let him fall out of the car

  4. He liked his job very much. It was very *unfortunate* when he lost it.
    a. superstitious
    b. unlucky

    c. lucky
    d. poor

5. He lost his old job, but the next day, he found a much better job. He was very *fortunate.*
    a. rich
    b. unlucky
    c. lucky
    d. a lot of money

6. He *considered* his choices before deciding what to do.
    a. thought about
    b. made a decision
    c. complained about
    d. talked about

7. She always thinks about her friends' and family's wishes before her own. She wants everyone to be comfortable and happy because she is a very *considerate* person.
    a. thoughtful and attentive
    b. attractive and smart
    c. intelligent and friendly
    d. selfish

8. That child often breaks his toys and *tears* his books and clothes. His parents always have to repair them.
    a. fixes paper or material
    b. cries very much
    c. bad conduct
    d. rips or damages paper or material

9. If you push that glass, it will *fall* off the table.
    a. move from the table to the floor
    b. move to the other side of the table
    c. break
    d. tear into many pieces

10. Halloween *falls* on a Wednesday this year.
    a. the middle of the week
    b. holiday
    c. does
    d. is

Word Forms

Sometimes, when a noun ends with the letters *-ion*, its adjective form ends with the letters *-ous*. For example:

superstition	superstitious
continuation	continuous
suspicion	suspicious
religion	religious
infection	infectious
pretention	pretentious

In a previous chapter, we learned that we can know if a word is an adjective or noun form by its position in a sentence. In the sentences below, decide if the adjective or noun form of the word is needed and write it in the blank spaces:

Example

superstition, superstitious

A ___*Superstitious*___ person probably believes many ___*Superstitions*___.

1. **continuation, continuous**

   The _____ heat is putting everyone in a bad mood. The _____ of this hot weather will drive us all crazy!

2. **suspicion, suspicious**

   I am _____ of his sincerity. My _____ is that he's not always honest.

3. **pretention, pretentious**

   He is a very _____ person! He has a lot of _____ about his abilities, which are really very few.

4. **religion, religious**

   _____ is a very important part of life in Saudi Arabia and some other countries. Almost all the people in these places are very _____.

5. **infection, infectious**

   An _____ can cause a cold or the flu. These are _____ illnesses which others can catch from us.

Group Activities

SMALL GROUP RETELLING OF READING PASSAGE AND DISCUSSION

Work with a small group of students. Each student in the group can tell a few of the superstitions mentioned in the reading passage until all of them have been retold. Try to use the present real conditional (*if . . . will*) structure when you describe the superstitions. Next, each student can describe superstitions in his or her country. One student can write down the superstitions in each country and later report them to the rest of the class.

Also, with the members of your group, discuss these questions: Are you superstitious? Are people in your country generally superstitious? Why do you think superstitions occur in so many places in the world? Why are people superstitious? Will people always be superstitious? Or, will people in the future stop believing superstitions?

ROLE-PLAYS

Divide the class into small groups or pairs. Each group or pair can choose one of the following situations to role-play for the rest of the class:

1. You are holding a mirror in your hand while brushing your hair or shaving. Suddenly you drop the mirror and it breaks. You have bad luck for the rest of the day. You miss your train; you are late for work; your boss is angry with you; you make mistakes at your job; you come home and have an argument with your husband or wife. Write a dialogue to role-play for the rest of the class.

2. You and your friend are walking on the street and you both approach a ladder. You are a superstitious person and you tell your friend not to walk under the ladder. But your friend says she is not superstitious, and walks under the ladder anyway. For the rest of the day, your friend has bad luck. What happens to your friend? What is her reaction to the bad luck? What is the conversation between you and your friend? Write some lines of dialogue to role-play for the rest of the class.

3. You and your friend are on a picnic. While sitting on the ground, you both see a four-leaf clover. You both want to take it. You argue about who saw it first. You decide that the person who has good luck for the rest of the day is the person who really saw it first and can keep it. What happens to you and to your friend for the rest of the day? Write some lines of dialogue to role-play for the rest of the class.

4. Did you or someone you know ever have good or bad luck as a result of a superstition? Role-play this situation for the rest of the class.

SIMON SAYS

Listen as your teacher tells you to perform the various actions mentioned in this chapter. Perform the actions only if your teacher first says the words *Simon says.* If you make a mistake, you must sit down and stop playing the game. The last person left standing is the winner.

Possible commands are:

Drop a mirror and break it.	Avoid walking under a ladder.
Pick up the broken pieces of the mirror—carefully!	Find a penny on the ground and pick it up.

PRACTICE WITH *EVEN*

The word *even* appears several times in the reading "Superstitions." Sometimes the meaning of this word is not immediately clear to students. We use the word *even* to *emphasize* a certain point, or to make the point stronger.

Look at the use of *even* in the sentences below:

1. Every society is a little bit superstitious—even societies that are very rational and scientific.
2. Almost any person can learn to use a computer—even a child.
3. Everyone says that man is a terrible person—even his own mother.
4. Everyone likes vacations from class sometimes—even teachers.
5. Many people avoid walking under ladders—even people who say they are not superstitious.

We can rewrite such sentences in the following way without changing the meaning:

Example

1. *Even societies that are very rational and scientific are a little bit superstitious.*

With the members of your group, rewrite sentences 2–5 in the same way:

2. _____

_____

3. _____

_____

4. _____

_____

5. _____

_____

chapter 9

Can I Stay at Your Place?

The Future with Going to

Pre-reading Questions

What are the responsibilities of a friend?

Should you help your friend in all situations?

If your friend has a problem, should you help him or her?

If your friend needs money, should you give it to him or her?

If your friend needs a place to stay, should you open your home to him or her?

Look at the pictures and tell what you see.

Many big American cities have housing problems. Often the cost of rent for apartments is very high. Sometimes, the cost of rent becomes so high that people can't afford their apartments anymore.

Below is a telephone conversation between two friends, Ellen and Karen. Ellen's landlord is going to raise the rent on her apartment and she cannot afford to pay it. Ellen tells her problem to Karen and asks her friend for help.

Can I Stay at Your Place?

Ellen: Karen? Hi, this is Ellen.

Karen: Oh, hi Ellen. How are you doing?

Ellen: Well, pretty bad. You won't believe what happened. The landlord is going to raise my rent another three hundred dollars a month! I can't afford that!

Karen: Oh, no, that's terrible! What are you going to do?

Ellen: I'm going to have to move to a new apartment. But it's going to take me a long time to find another place. Where am I going to go? All the apartments in this city are so expensive these days.

Karen: That's for sure. Boy, soon this city is going to be only for rich people. It's an awful situation. I really feel sorry for you, Ellen. I wish I could help you.

Ellen: Well, as a matter of fact, Karen, I am going to ask you for a favor.

Karen: What is it?

Ellen: Well . . . uh . . . do you think . . . maybe I could stay at your place for a while? Just until I find another apartment . . . and straighten things out?

Karen: Well, uh, Ellen, you know I'd love to say yes, but . . . I'm going to be very honest with you. I don't think it will work out if you stay here. I'm going to be really busy with school and work in the next few weeks and I'm going to need my privacy. I'm sorry, Ellen, but I'm going to have to say no.

Ellen: Well, Karen, I'm going to be very honest with you, too. I don't think you're a very good friend. You're so selfish! You don't care about anybody but yourself! I'm your best friend and you're not even going to help me. You're just going to pretend my problem doesn't exist! I guess our friendship doesn't matter to you.

Karen: Oh, Ellen, of course our friendship matters to me! But I think it will be bad for our friendship if you stay at my place. If we're together all the time, we won't get along.

Ellen: It's bad enough I'm going to lose my apartment. I guess I'm going to lose my best friend, too. With friends like you, I don't need enemies. I'm not going to talk to you anymore. I'm going to hang up the phone!

Karen: Please don't hang up, Ellen! Listen to me—

Ellen: I'm not going to listen to you if you're not going to act like a friend. Are you going to help me or not?

What do you think Karen is going to say? What is going to happen?

Listen as your teacher reads the following statements, and tell if they are true or false:

1. In some big American cities, apartments are becoming more and more expensive.
2. Sometimes people have trouble paying their rent.
3. Karen's landlord is going to raise her rent.
4. Ellen can afford to pay the new rent.
5. Ellen asks Karen for help.
6. Ellen thinks she can find a new apartment quickly.
7. Apartments in Ellen's city are becoming more and more expensive.
8. Ellen wants to move into Karen's apartment permanently.
9. Karen agrees that Ellen can stay at her place for a while.
10. Karen says she is going to be very busy in the next few weeks and needs time to be alone.
11. Ellen accepts Karen's decision.
12. Karen gets angry with Ellen.
13. Ellen thinks Karen doesn't care about their friendship.
14. Karen tells Ellen that she is going to hang up the phone.
15. Karen thinks that she and Ellen will get along very well if they live together.

The Future with going to

We use the verb *to be* with *going to* and the base form of the main verb to express a future action:

subject	verb *to be*	*going to*	main verb base form
I	am	going to	move.
You (we, they)	are	going to	move.
He (she, it)	is	going to	move.

To form a question, we reverse the position of the subject and the verb *to be*:

verb *to be*	subject	*going to*	main verb base form
Am	I	going to	move?
Are	you (we, they)	going to	move?
Is	he (she, it)	going to	move?

To make a negative statement, we put *not* after the verb *to be*:

subject	verb *to be*	*not*	*going to*	main verb base form
I	am	not	going to	move.
You (we, they)	are	not	going to	move.
He (she, it)	is	not	going to	move.

Often, we put the subject together with the verb *to be* to form the following contractions:

I + am = I'm	he + is = he's	we + are = we're
you + are = you're	she + is = she's	they + are = they're
	it + is = it's	

Often, we put the verb *to be* and *not* together to form the following contractions:

is + not = isn't   are + not = aren't

PRACTICE WITH *GOING TO*: MAKING PREDICTIONS

What is going to happen between Karen and Ellen?

In the spaces below, write the correct form of the verb *to be* with *going to* and the appropriate base form of the main verb. Do not use the same verb more than one time.

change   get along   help   keep   let   work out

Example

a. Karen *is going to change* _____ her mind about the situation.

1. Karen ————————————— Ellen.
2. Karen —————————————————Ellen stay in her apartment.
3. The two friends ————————————————if they live together.
4. Karen ————————————— Ellen's friendship.
5. The situation ——————————————— between the two friends.

Now write the above sentences with *not* to make the opposite predictions:

Example

b. Karen *is not going to change* her mind about the situation.

6. Karen ————————————— Ellen.
7. Karen —————————————————Ellen stay in her apartment.
8. The two friends ————————————————if they live together.
9. Karen ————————————— Ellen's friendship.
10. The situation ——————————————— between the two friends.

Vocabulary

Write the appropriate verbs in the spaces provided. Do not use the same verb more than one time.

act	guess	matter	raise
afford	hang up	move	straighten out
exist	have to	pretend	work out
feel sorry for			

Example

a. Ellen can't _afford_____ to pay the high rent on her apartment.

1. We sold our old house. We are going to _move_____ to our new house next week.

2. That poor family has so many problems! I _feel sorry for_ them.

3. This restaurant is becoming more and more expensive! Every week the owner _raises_____ the prices on the menu!

4. She doesn't really like his apartment. She just _pretend_ to like it to be polite.

5. If you don't pay your rent, you are going to _have to_ move out of this apartment!

6. I don't really know exactly how much rent he pays. I _guess_____ he pays about $600 a month for his apartment.

7. Please don't _hang up_ the phone yet. I want to tell you something else.

8. You're not a mature person. You're an adult, but you _act_____ like a child!

9. It doesn't _matter_____ if you pay your rent late. Everyone in this building pays the rent late, and the landlord doesn't care.

10. I don't think his new job is going to _straighten out_ so well. He doesn't like it, and he argues with his boss.

11. I'm sure you can _work out_____ your problems. You won't have them forever.

12. Every apartment in this building is very expensive. Cheap apartments don't _exist_____ here.

Now supply the appropriate noun.

apartment	favor	place
cost	friendship	privacy
enemy	landlord	rent

Example

b. My **apartment** has one bedroom, a living room, and a kitchen.

13. The _____cost_____ of living in big cities is getting more expensive all the time.

14. The _____rent_____ on that apartment is $500 a month.

15. An _____enemy_____ is the opposite of a friend.

16. She is a very popular person, and has _____friendships_____ with many people.

17. Our _____landlord_____ owns three other buildings, too.

18. We had dinner at your apartment last week. Let's eat at my _____place_____ this week.

19. He doesn't like to spend a lot of time with other people. His _____privacy_____ is very important to him.

20. Can you please do me a _____favor_____? Help me clean the house.

Now supply the appropriate adjective.

awful	high	pretty
best	honest	selfish
busy	housing	**terrible**

Example

c. His apartment has no light, no hot water, broken floors, and windows. It's a _**terrible**_ place to live.

21. The _____ situation in New York City is a real problem. It's very difficult to find inexpensive places to live.

22. I have so much work to do! I'm going to be very _____busy_____ for the next few weeks.

23. I'm _____pretty_____ happy these days. Most things in my life are going well.

24. He has an _____ apartment. It's small and dark and dirty.

25. I can't afford to buy anything in this store because the prices are too _high_.

26. An _honest_ person tells the truth.

27. There are a lot of very good restaurants in this city, but this one is really the _best_ of all.

28. He cares only about himself. He never considers other people's feelings. He's a very _selfish_ person.

Now supply the appropriate preposition. You may use the same word more than one time.

at   between   **for**   in   of   to   until

Example
d. She's going to look _for_ another apartment.

29. The cost _____ living in many places is becoming more expensive.

30. He's going to stay _in_ a hotel during his vacation.

31. Can I ask you _for_ a favor?

32. Every apartment _until_ this building costs $600 a month or more.

33. Please don't tell that story to anyone else. It's just _between_ you and me.

34. He can't afford _to_ buy a new house now.

35. Let's have coffee _____ it's time for class.

36. I bought new chairs _for_ my apartment.

Dictation/Cloze

Listen as your teacher reads, and write the words that you hear in the blanks.

Ellen's landlord _____ _____ _____
                             1   2   3

_____ her rent by three hundred dollars a month. Ellen can't
      4

_____ this new rent, so she _____ _____
      5   6   7

_____ _____ for another apartment. However, she
      8   9

_____ _____ _____ _____ a place to
      10   11   12   13

stay _____ she finds a new apartment. Ellen asks her friend
           14

Karen if she can stay _____ her place. But Karen says that she
                            15

_____ _____ _____ _____ very busy
      16   17   18   19

for the next few weeks. She _____ _____ _____
                                  20   21   22

_____ a lot of _____. Karen doesn't think it _____
      23   24   25

_____ _____ _____ _____ if Ellen
      26   27   28   29

lives with her. Ellen becomes very angry and says she _____
                                                            30

_____ _____ _____ _____ Karen any-
      31   32   33   34

more if Karen _____ _____ _____ _____
                    35   36   37   38

her.

   What do you think _____ _____ _____
                           39   40   41

_____ between the two friends?
      42

Reading Comprehension

Circle the letter of the correct answers to the following questions.

1. The main idea of this reading passage is:
   a. Apartments are too expensive everywhere.
   b. It's hard to live with another person.

   c. Landlords want too much money these days.

   d. The housing problem causes two friends to face the responsibilities and limits of their friendship.

2. A detail of this reading is:

   a. Karen has a very small apartment.

   b. Karen is a selfish person.

   c. Ellen expected her best friend Karen to let her stay at her apartment, but Karen wouldn't agree to this.

   d. Ellen should straighten out her own problems and not depend on
others.

3. According to the reading, which of the following sentences is true?

   a. Karen is angry with Ellen for asking a favor.

   b. Ellen wants Karen to give her some money for her high rent.

   c. Karen is afraid that she and Ellen won't get along if they live
together.

   d. Ellen wants to live with Karen permanently.

4. According to the reading, which of the following sentences is *not*
true?

   a. Karen and Ellen are best friends.

   b. Karen is going to have a lot of things to do in the next few weeks.

   c. Ellen is going to have to pay another thirty-six hundred dollars
rent each year.

   d. Ellen thinks it will be very easy to find another apartment.

5. In your opinion, based on the reading, which of the following sentences is true?

   a. The cost of living in Ellen's city is not high.

   b. Karen doesn't care about her friendship with Ellen.

   c. Karen has a lot of free time.

   d. Ellen is not very wealthy.

6. Which pair has the words that are most similar in meaning?

   a. *hang up* and *good-bye*

   b. *awful* and *terrible*

   c. *rent* and *cost*

   d. *selfish* and *lonely*

Guessing Meanings from Context

Guess the meanings of the italicized words from the context. Circle the
letter of the words that are most similar in meaning to the italicized
word(s):

Example

Ellen's landlord is going to *raise* her rent an additional $300 a month.
Ⓐ increase
b. decrease
c. cost
d. more

1. When landlords raise the rent, the *tenants* have to pay more money.
   a. students
   b. families
   c. people who rent the apartments
   d. people who want to change apartments

2. Believe it or not, my friend's landlord is going to *lower* his rent from $600 a month to $550. What a lucky tenant my friend is!
   a. fortunate
   b. slow
   c. raise
   d. decrease

3. Often, when a person rents an apartment, he or she has to sign a one- or two-year *lease.*
   a. mailbox
   b. lock
   c. a paper that says you will buy your apartment in one or two years
   d. a paper that says you agree to rent the apartment for one or two years

4. When you finish your telephone conversation, please *hang up* the phone.
   a. put down the telephone receiver
   b. pick up the telephone receiver
   c. drop the telephone receiver
   d. say goodbye

5. After you get undressed, please *hang up* your clothes.
   a. take off your clothes
   b. put on your clothes
   c. put down the telephone receiver
   d. put your clothes on hangers or hooks

6. The dinner wasn't great, but it was *pretty* good.
   a. (good) enough
   b. very

    c. beautiful
    d. absolutely delicious

7. Many actresses have very *pretty* faces and figures.
    a. attractive
    b. skinny
    c. theater
    d. plays

8. I think you will *work out* your problems. Soon, everything will be all right.
    a. work hard
    b. work outdoors
    c. solve
    d. forget

9. He wants his body to be in good condition, so he *works out* at the gym every morning.
    a. eats a big breakfast
    b. stays healthy
    c. gets up early
    d. exercises

10. I always tell my best friend my problems. I *trust* her to help me.
    a. have confidence in; depend on
    b. talk
    c. tell the truth
    d. like very much

Word Forms

We remember from previous chapters that a *suffix* is a group of letters at the end of a word that *modifies*, or changes, the meaning of the word. There are many different suffixes in English. One example is *-less*, which means "without." If we put *-less* at the end of a word, it adds the meaning "without." For example, the word *hopeless* means "without hope." The word *sleeveless* means "without sleeves."

    Another common suffix is *-ship*. This means "the quality or state of something." If we put *-ship* at the end of a word, it adds this meaning. For example, the word *friendship* means "the quality or state of being friends."

    On the next page are some more examples of words that can take the *-ship* suffix.

champion—championship   sportsman—sportsmanship
citizen—citizenship   workman—workmanship
relation—relationship

In the sentences below, decide which form of the word is needed, and write in the space provided. In each case, the first word describes a certain kind of person; the second word describes a certain kind of quality or state.

Example

friend, friendship

Bob is my best *friend*____. Our *friendship* will last forever.

1. **citizen, citizenship**

   He wants to be an American _____. If he passes the exam, he will get his _____.

2. **relation, relationship**

   We have a big, happy family with a lot of brothers, sisters, aunts, cousins, and other _____. We all have a great _____ with each other.

3. **sportsman, sportsmanship**

   A good _____ doesn't get angry if he loses a tennis game or some other sports event. He practices good _____.

4. **workman, workmanship**

   Look at the beautiful _____on this table! The _____ who made it was a very talented man.

5. **champion, championship**

   Our baseball team won the _____ this year! Every person on our team is a _____.

Group Activities

SMALL GROUP RETELLING OF STORY AND DISCUSSION

Work with a small group of students. Each student in the group can tell a little of the story of Ellen and Karen until the entire story has been retold. After that, each student can give his or her opinion of the story. How is the telephone conversation going to end? Is Karen going to change her mind? Is she going to let Ellen stay with her? Is Ellen going to stop being angry? Is she going to understand Karen's situation? Also consider:

1. What do you think a friend should do in this situation? Should Karen let Ellen stay with her? Is this her responsibility as Ellen's best friend?

2. When a situation like this happens in your country, what do most people do? Do they always permit friends to stay with them? What do you think most American people do?

3. If you are in a situation like this one day, what will you do?

4. In your country, do most people live in apartments or houses? Do they usually rent them or own them? Are they expensive? Is housing generally becoming more and more expensive in your country? Do people sometimes have problems like Ellen's?

ROLE-PLAYS

Divide the students into pairs. Each pair can choose one of the following situations to role-play for the rest of the class:

1. Finish the telephone conversation between Ellen and Karen. Write about five or six more lines of dialogue. Then, go to the front of the class and read the entire dialogue, including the lines you wrote. Don't just read. First, look at the lines, then look up and *speak* them to your partner.

2. After several pairs of students have gone to the front of the class and read the dialogue, you and your partner can go to the front of your class *without* your book and act out the story. It's not necessary to use the same words that are in the dialogue (though you may if you remember them). You can act out the situation using your own words, too.

3. Imagine another argument between two friends over the telephone (or between a boyfriend and girlfriend, or a husband and wife). Write a dialogue and role-play it for the rest of the class. Be sure to include in your dialogue some of these common telephone expressions:

May I speak to _____?	I dialed wrong.
Is _____ there?	You have the wrong number.
This is _____.	I have to go now.
Hold on, please.	I'll let you go now.

Just a minute, please.   Don't hang up yet.
I'll call you back later.

WRITING EXERCISE

Did you ever have a problem with a good friend? Tell the rest of the class about this problem. When you have finished, the other students can write about it.

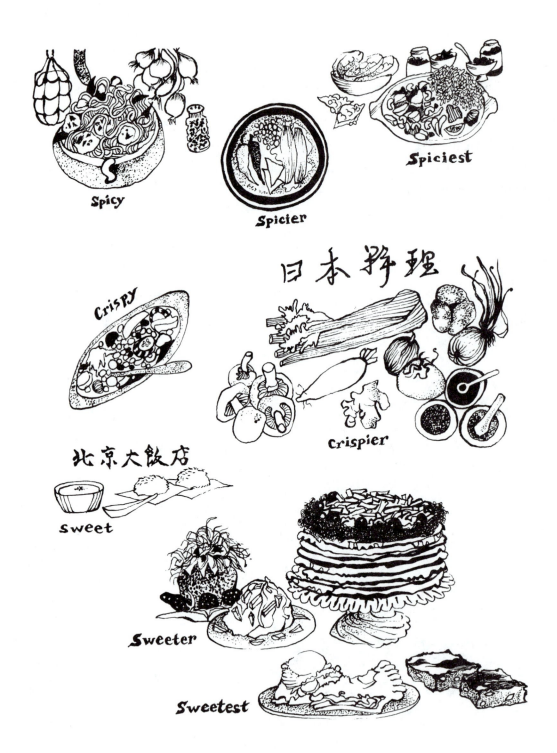

Spicy

Spicier

Spiciest

日本料理

Crispy

Crispier

北京大飯店

sweet

Sweeter

Sweetest

chapter 10

Food Near and Far

Comparative and Superlative Adjectives

Pre-reading Questions

Look at the pictures and tell what you see.

What is your favorite food?

Do you like American food?

Do you like food from your native country better than American-style food?

Food Near and Far

Everyone loves to eat! People in every country enjoy this activity.[1] There are so many different kinds of food in the world—there is Chinese food, Italian food, South American food, Indian food, and many others.[2] It's fun to eat and compare the different types of cuisine.[3] Italian food is sometimes very spicy, but South American food is usually much spicier.[4] Indian food can be the spiciest food of all[5]—sometimes it's so hot that it can make your mouth burn![6] But that's okay because then you can drink some good Italian or French or California wine to soothe the burning![7]

Some wonderful food comes from the Oriental countries. Chinese food is popular in many parts of the world. Lots of people love Chinese-style vegetables because they are so crispy.[8] Because we cook Chinese-style vegetables for a much shorter time, they are crispier than American-style vegetables.[9] In fact, they are probably the crispiest cooked vegetables you can find.[10]

It's always fun to eat desserts.[11] Desserts in Oriental countries are often less sweet than desserts in Western countries.[12] For example, European cakes and pastries are richer and sweeter than Chinese custard or Japanese rice cakes.[13]

The United States has some of the sweetest desserts you can find—apple pie with ice cream, banana splits, and chocolate brownies, to name a few.[14]

Some people don't like American-style food.[15] They think it is often less tasty and sometimes less nutritious than food in other countries.[16] Americans eat more "fast food" than people in other countries.[17] Fast foods take a short time to prepare. Hamburgers, hot dogs, pizza, canned and frozen food are all examples of fast foods.[18] Often, Americans feel they are too busy to spend a lot of time cooking.[19]

Of course, in some other countries, like France, cooking is still an "art form."[20] Some people believe that French cuisine is the best in the world.[21] Certainly, each person has a different opinion about which country has the tastiest food. But people in many places agree that French food is the most delicious and the best-prepared.[22]

1. What do people in every country love to do?
2. What are some of the different kinds of food in the world?
3. What is it fun to do?
4. Compare Italian food and South American food.
5. Compare Italian food, South American food, and Indian food.
6. What can Indian food do to you?
7. What can you do to soothe the burning?
8. What do lots of people love?
9. Compare Chinese-style vegetables and American-style vegetables.
10. Are other vegetables crispier than Chinese-style vegetables?

11. What is it always fun to eat?
12. Are desserts in every country the same?
13. Are European-style desserts the same as Japanese or Chinese-style desserts?
14. What kinds of desserts does the United States have? What are some examples of these desserts?
15. Does everyone like American-style food?
16. What do some people think of American-style food?
17. What do Americans eat more of?
18. What are "fast foods"? What are some examples of fast foods?
19. What do Americans often feel?
20. What is true about cooking in some other countries?
21. What do some people believe?
22. Does every person have the same opinion about French cooking?
23. Which country's cuisine is your favorite?

Comparative and Superlative Adjectives

We use the *comparative* form of an adjective when we compare two nouns. In general, we form the comparative by adding -*er* to a short word (one or two syllables), or by putting *more* in front of a long word (two, three or more syllables):

subject	verb *to be*	adjective + -*er* *more* + adjective	than	object
Cake	is	sweeter	than	bread.
French food	is	more delicious	than	American food.

We use the *superlative* form of an adjective when we compare one noun to two or more other nouns. In general, we form the superlative by adding -*est* to a short word (one or two syllables), or by putting *the most* in front of a long word (two, three or more syllables):

subject	verb *to be*	adjective + -*est* *the most* + adjective	of all	object
Brownies	are	the sweetest	of all	these cakes.
French food	is	the most delicious	of all	the foods.

NOTE: The opposite of *more* is *less*. The opposite of *the most* is *the least*. Note the following irregular comparatives:

base	comparative	superlative
good	better	the best
bad	worse	the worst

Note the spelling changes in the following two-syllable adjectives ending in *-y*:

base	comparative	superlative
spicy	spicier	the spiciest
crispy	crispier	the crispiest
salty	saltier	the saltiest
tasty	tastier	the tastiest
healthy	healthier	the healthiest

PRACTICE WITH ADJECTIVE FORMS: MAKING COMPARISONS

Write the comparative form (-er, more, less) of the adjective noted under the blanks to express your opinion about the food comparisons in the following sentences:

Examples

a. American desserts are __*sweeter*__ than Chinese desserts.
   (sweet)

b. Brownies are __*more delicious*__ than apple pie.
   (delicious)

c. North American food is __*less spicy*__ than South American food.
   (spicy)

1. Italian food is _____ than Chinese food.
   (tasty)

2. Japanese food is _____ than American fast food.
   (nutritious)

3. Mexican food is _____ than French food.
   (spicy)

4. American-style vegetables are _____ than Oriental-style vegetables.
   (crispy)

5. Italian food is _____ than Japanese food.
   (fattening)

6. American food is _____ than Chinese food.
   (delicious)

7. Candy is _____ than fruit.
   (sweet)

8. Ham is _____ than chicken.
   (salty)

Now write the superlative forms (*-est*, the most, the least) of the adjectives below to express your opinion about the foods in the following sentences. Use a different adjective for each answer.

bad	fattening	salty	sweet
crispy	good	**spicy**	tasty
delicious	hot		

Examples

a. Indian food is *the spiciest* food of all.

b. Apple pie is *the most delicious* dessert of all.

c. Fish is *the least tasty* food of all.

9. American food is _____ food of all.

10. Italian pasta and cheese dishes are _____ _____ dishes of all.

11. Mexican food is _____ of all Latin American food.

12. Chinese-style vegetables are _____ of all.

13. Japanese raw fish is _____ food of all.

Vocabulary

Write the appropriate verbs in the spaces provided. Do not use the same verb more than one time.

be fun (to)	cook	**love**	spend time
burn	eat	make	take time
compare	enjoy	soothe	

Example

a. I *love* ice cream! It's my favorite food of all.

1. Fran always _____ too much when she goes to an Italian restaurant. She loves Italian food!

2. Let's _____ the two restaurants. Which restaurant is better?

3. I need some water! That hot Mexican food _____ my mouth!

4. The poor child burned his hand on the hot stove. Put some ice on his hand to _____ the pain.

5. The chef is going to _____ a special French dish tonight.

6. It _____ to eat foods from different countries. Everyone likes to try new dishes.

7. It _____ a long _____ to prepare a good South American dinner.

8. They _____ a long _____ preparing dinner. It took them almost three hours!

9. Very spicy food _____ my stomach upset.

10. We always _____ the dinners you cook. They are just delicious!

Now supply the appropriate noun.

activity	burning	custard	opinion
art form	chef	dessert	pastries
banana split	cooking	favorite	
brownie	cuisine	**ice cream**	

Example
b. After dinner, there is *ice cream* for dessert.

11. The _____ of this restaurant cooks very creative, original dishes.

12. I love all different kinds of desserts, but especially chocolate cake. It's my _____ of all the desserts.

13. A _____ is a small square of rich, delicious chocolate cake.

14. A _____ is three scoops of ice cream, whipped cream, nuts, and fruit between two slices of a banana.

15. _____ is made with milk, eggs, and sugar.

16. I ate too much spicy Mexican food. My mouth is on fire! Give me some water to stop the _____!

17. He does all the _____ for his family. He makes breakfast, lunch, and dinner every day.

18. Which country has the best _____? Each person has a different _____.

19. French _____ are a wonderful dessert. They are especially good with coffee.

20. He loves to cook. Cooking is his favorite _____.

21. Dance, music, and painting are some examples of _____.

Now supply the appropriate adjective.

best	frozen	Oriental	sweet
canned	hot	rich	tasty
crispy	nutritious	spicy	Western
delicious			

> **Example**
> c. This is the most _*delicious*_ dessert on the menu. Everyone loves it the best.

22. Sugar is _____, but salt isn't.

23. This restaurant is great! It's the _____ of all the restaurants in the city.

24. Mexican food is really very _____. Sometimes it's so _____ that it makes your mouth burn.

25. These vegetables are very _____. Everyone wants more!

26. In general, _____ desserts are sweeter than _____ desserts.

27. Apples are a _____ fruit, but bananas aren't.

28. A banana split is a very _____ dessert. It's full of sugar, cream, and calories!

29. Fruits and vegetables are good for the body. They are very _____ foods.

30. We need a dessert that takes a short time to prepare. Let's open some _____ fruit.

31. We don't have time to cut and prepare fresh vegetables. Open the refrigerator and take out a box of _____ vegetables. We can make them quickly.

Now supply the appropriate preposition. You may use the same word more than one time.

     about   in   **of**   to

Example
d. We ate Italian food lots _*of*_ times last year.

32. I love Japanese food. _____ fact, I eat it more often than any other type _____ food.

33. We like to eat _____ different kinds _____ restaurants.

34. He knows many things _____ French cooking. A few years ago, he was a chef _____ a French restaurant.

35. If you want the vegetables to be crispy, cook them only _____ five minutes.

36. He loves to eat apple pie with ice cream. He ate all _____ his dessert, and all _____ my dessert, too!

Dictation/Cloze

Listen as your teacher reads, and write the words that you hear in the blank spaces:

It's fun to _____ the foods of different countries. Every country _____ the world _____ its own special
_____. South American food is usually _____ _____
North American food. Mexican food is really _____. It is perhaps
_____ _____ of all Latin American food.

Chinese food is usually _____ _____ _____
Mexican food. Chinese food is _____ popular _____
many parts _____ the world. Many people think that Chinese-
style vegetables are _____ and _____ _____
American-style vegetables. Chinese food is often _____
_____ _____ American food because it has _____
sugar and starch.

American desserts are often _____ _____ Chinese
desserts and Oriental desserts in general. Americans eat _____
cakes, pies, and ice cream _____ people in Oriental countries do.

Some people say that French desserts are _____ _____
_____ in the world. Many people consider French chefs
_____ _____ in the world. People in many parts of the
world love French cuisine.

Of course, each person has a different opinion about _____

_____ cuisine in the world. Everyone has a _____. In
             33   34

your opinion, what is _____ _____ _____ cui-
                                        35   36   37

sine?

Reading Comprehension

Circle the letter of the correct answers to the following questions.

1. The main idea of this reading passage is:
   a. American food is less delicious than food in other countries.
   b. People in many countries like Chinese food.
   c. It's interesting and fun to make a comparison of foods in different countries.
   d. Many people like to eat.

2. A detail of this reading passage is:
   a. South American food is spicier than North American food.
   b. Everyone likes to drink wine.
   c. Wine makes your mouth burn.
   d. French chefs love to eat desserts.

3. Which of the following sentences is true according to the reading passage?
   a. French food is delicious, but not well-prepared.
   b. Chinese food is the best food in the world.
   c. Italian food is usually less spicy than South American food.
   d. Japanese desserts are often sweeter than American desserts.

4. Which of the following sentences is *not* true according to the reading passage?
   a. Everyone in the world likes French food the best.
   b. Many people in the world believe French cuisine is the best, but there are people who prefer other types of cooking.
   c. In general, desserts in some countries are sweeter and richer than desserts in other countries.
   d. It's fun to compare foods in different countries.

5. In your opinion, based on the reading passage, which of the following sentences is true?
   a. The United States has the best food.
   b. American desserts are more nutritious than desserts in other countries.

    c. American desserts don't use a lot of sugar.

    d. Many Americans don't like to spend a lot of their time preparing meals every day.

6. Which pair has the words that are most similar in meaning?

    a. *delicious* and *nutritious*

    b. *hot* and *burn*

    c. *favorite* and *best*

    d. *very spicy* and *hot*

Guessing Meanings from Context

Guess the meanings of the italicized words from the context. Circle the letter of the word or words that are most similar in meaning to the italicized word(s):

Example

Mexican food contains a lot of spices. North American people think it's very *hot.*

    a. opposite of "cold"

    b. warm

    c. not tasty

    d. spicy

1. Oranges are sweet, but lemons are *sour.*

    a. very sweet

    b. opposite of "sweet"

    c. tasty

    d. small

2. If you eat a *healthful* diet, you won't get sick very often.

    a. delicious

    b. hot

    c. nutritious

    d. rich

3. For breakfast, I want *fried* eggs. First, break the eggs, then fry them in a hot pan.

    a. broken

    b. French

    c. cooked in hot water

    d. cooked in hot butter or oil

4. Tomorrow, I want a couple of *boiled* eggs for breakfast. Put two whole eggs into a pot and cook them for a few minutes.
   a. broken
   b. cooked in very, very hot water
   c. cooked in hot oil
   d. fried

5. Give me a *well-done* steak for dinner. I don't want it red. I want it very brown.
   a. well-prepared
   b. cooked for a short time
   c. cooked for a long time
   d. delicious

6. My friend wants a *rare* steak. He doesn't want it brown. He wants it very red.
   a. dark
   b. color
   c. cooked for a long time
   d. cooked for a short time

7. Most of the time, we eat dinner at home. It's *rare* for us to eat at restaurants.
   a. often
   b. usual
   c. unusual
   d. cooked for a short time

8. Give me a big *slice* of pizza. I'm hungry today.
   a. pie
   b. Italian food
   c. fast food
   d. piece

9. *Slice* the pizza eight ways. Eight people want to share it.
   a. cut
   b. piece
   c. give
   d. tear

10. This soup is too *hot*. Let's wait a few moments before we eat it.
    a. spicy
    b. burn
    c. opposite of "cold"
    d. Mexican

Word Forms

In previous chapters, we learned that a word that ends with *-ing* can be a noun or an adjective, depending on its position in the sentence. In "Food Near and Far" we see that a word with an *-ing* ending can also be a noun. For example: "But that's okay because then you can drink some wine to soothe *the burning*." (Remember that nouns are often preceded by articles.)

In the sentences below, decide if the words with *-ing* endings are nouns, verbs, or adjectives. Write *n*, *v*, or *a* next to each sentence. Be ready to explain your choices.

Examples

a. The soup is *cooking* on the stove.   V
b. I love the smell of *cooking* soup.   A
c. I'll do the *cooking* tonight.   N

1. We're *boiling* some eggs for breakfast.   _____
2. We put three eggs into *boiling* water.   _____
3. Stop the *boiling* after three minutes.   _____

4. She does all the *baking* for our family.   _____
5. She's *baking* bread today.   _____
6. That *baking* bread smells wonderful!   _____

7. The potatoes are *frying* in the pan.   _____
8. You cut the potatoes. I'll do the *frying*.   _____
9. Listen to the sound of those *frying* potatoes!   _____

10. Look at that smoke! The building is *burning!*   _____
11. The firemen are entering the *burning* building.   _____
12. They are trying hard to stop the *burning*.   _____

13. He's not a *drinking* man. He never drinks alcohol—only soft drinks.   _____
14. My brother is *drinking* another glass of wine.   _____
15. He should stop that *drinking!* All that wine isn't good for him.   _____

Group Activities

SMALL GROUP RETELLING AND DISCUSSION OF READING

Work with a small group of students. Each student in the group can tell a little of the information in the reading until all the information has been retold. Be sure to use the correct form of the comparative and superlative adjectives in your retelling.

Also, with the members of your group, discuss these questions: What are your favorite foods? Compare foods in your native country to foods in the United States (or to foods in your classmates' native countries). For example, you might compare:

vegetable dishes   desserts
meat and fish dishes   fruits

DESCRIBING AND GUESSING

Write a description of an American food. Don't write the name of the food—just describe it. Read your description to the rest of the class. The other students can guess the food. For example:

> This food is large and round. It has tomato sauce and cheese on top of a thin bread crust. It's spicy. You always eat this food hot, not cold. You cut it into six or eight slices, and usually eat one or two of them (or more if you're very hungry). What is this food?

ROLE-PLAYS

Divide the class into pairs or small groups. Each pair or group can choose one of the following situations to role-play for the rest of the class:

1. An American friend visits you and your family in your native country. One night, the American wants to cook one of your country's special dishes, but doesn't know how. You explain what to do and the American follows your instructions. Sometimes he or she makes some mistakes, and you have to correct these. Write some lines of dialogue to role-play for the rest of the class.

2. You and a friend are in a restaurant. You ask the waiter for boiled eggs, but he brings you scrambled eggs. Your friend asks the waiter for a rare hamburger, but the waiter brings a well-done hamburger. You and your friend tell the waiter his mistakes, but he insists he gave both of you what you asked for. You and your friend argue with him. Write some lines of dialogue to role-play for the rest of the class.

3. You go to a very elegant dinner party. The dinner is delicious! All the guests tell the host that the cooking is wonderful. Then, the host serves the dessert. It's a big, beautiful cake. But it doesn't taste sweet. It tastes salty! The host made the cake with salt instead of sugar by mistake! What do the guests say? Do they tell the host? Do they tell each other? What is the conversation? Write some lines of dialogue to role-play for the rest of the class.

DICTATION

Write a recipe for a dish from your native country. Then, dictate this recipe to the rest of the class. When you finish, each student in the class can dictate a line of the recipe back to you, and you can write it on the blackboard. The students can look at the blackboard and correct their mistakes.

SIMON SAYS

Listen as your teacher tells you to perform various actions. Perform the actions only if your teacher first says the words *Simon says*. If you make a mistake, you must sit down and stop playing the game.

Some possible commands are:

Slice some bread.
Bite an apple.
Cook some soup.
Eat some soup.
Eat a lemon.
Eat an ice cream cone.

Eat some very, very, very spicy food.
Drink a cup of coffee or tea that has ten spoonfuls of sugar in it.

chapter 11

An English Teacher Asks Her Students for Advice

The Unreal Conditional: If . . . Would

Pre-reading Questions

Did your English teacher ever study a foreign language?

Did he or she find it easy or difficult to learn this language?

Do you think it is always easy for English teachers to learn other languages?

What advice would you give to a person who wanted to learn your native language quickly?

Look at the pictures and tell what you see.

An English Teacher Asks Her Students for Advice

My name is Ann Kennedy and I'm an English teacher.[1] I really like my job.[2] It's a lot of fun to watch my students learn more and more English every day.[3] I feel very glad when they begin to feel comfortable speaking English. But I have to admit that sometimes I feel a little envious, too.[4] I would be so happy if I spoke a foreign language! But it's always been very hard for me to learn one.[5] When I was a university student, I studied Japanese for a few months. The Japanese language and culture fascinated me.[6] So, after the university, I made a trip to Japan.[7] I thought that if the Japanese language surrounded me, I would learn it quickly.[8] As soon as I arrived in Tokyo, I registered for a Japanese class which I attended every morning.[9] Outside of class, I tried to have conversations in Japanese.[10] But it wasn't easy! Although I could usually ask questions in Japanese, I never understood the answers I received![11] The Japanese people were always very kind and helpful, but I felt like a deaf person when they spoke to me![12] I understood almost nothing of what they said.[13] Sometimes I tried to translate from Japanese to English, but then I got even more confused and frustrated.[14]

When I spoke Japanese, I always felt nervous because I was afraid I would make a lot of mistakes if I didn't think carefully enough.[15] Also, my bad Japanese pronunciation embarrassed me. I was sure my American accent sounded terrible.[16]

There was another problem, too. Words in foreign languages never felt "real" to me. English words feel real to me because English is my native language, but Japanese words are just sounds.[17]

It was all too hard for me! I didn't feel I could express my personality in Japanese. I couldn't make jokes or say anything clever.[18] Finally, I gave up trying to learn the language. Some of the Japanese people I met spoke English very well, so I began to speak to them in English all the time.[19]

Of course, the day I returned to the United States, I didn't know much more Japanese than I had known the day I arrived in Tokyo.[20] I felt very disappointed in myself.[21]

Next summer, I'm planning to go to Japan again.[22] I'm going to spend about three months there.[23] This time, I really want to learn more Japanese![24] I don't want to come home feeling disappointed again.[25] But I'm afraid I'll have the same fears and make the same mistakes as last time.[26] What can I do to prevent this? Perhaps I'll ask my students for some advice.

1. Who is Ann Kennedy?
2. Does she like her job?
3. Why does she like her job?
4. How does Ann feel when her students begin to feel better about speaking English?

5. Why does Ann feel envious?
6. Did Ann ever study a foreign language?
7. Where did she go after the university?
8. What did Ann think?
9. What did Ann do when she arrived in Tokyo?
10. What else did she do?
11. What problem did Ann have?
12. How did she feel when the Japanese people spoke to her?
13. Did Ann always understand them?
14. What did Ann try to do sometimes? How did she feel?
15. How did Ann feel when she spoke Japanese? Why?
16. Why else was Ann nervous?
17. What was Ann's other problem?
18. What other difficulties did Ann have?
19. Did Ann continue to speak Japanese?
20. Did she know a lot more Japanese the day she returned to the United States?
21. How did Ann feel that day?
22. What's happening next summer?
23. How long is Ann going to spend in Japan?
24. What does Ann want to do this time?
25. What doesn't she want to do?
26. What is Ann afraid of?
27. What would you do if you were Ann Kennedy?

The Unreal Conditional: **If . . . Would**

We use the unreal conditional form (*if . . . would*) to describe imaginary situations in which one condition depends on another:

if	subject	past tense verb	object/complement
If	I	spoke	a foreign language,

subject	would	infinitive verb	object/complement
I	would	be	happy.

To make a question, we reverse the positions of *would* and the subject in the main clause. The *if* clause remains the same:

if	subject	past tense verb	object/complement
If	I	spoke	a foreign language,

would	subject	infinitive verb	object/complement
would	I	be	happy?

To form the negative, we follow the rule for past tense negative in the *if* clause, and put *not* after *would* in the main clause:

if	subject	didn't	infinitive verb	object/complement
If	I	didn't	speak	a foreign language,

subject	would	not	infinitive verb	object/complement
I	would (wouldn't)	not	be	happy.

Often, we put *would* and *not* together to form the following contraction:

would + not = wouldn't

When we use the verb *to be* in the *if* clause, we use *were* for *all* persons:

If I (you, he, she, it, we, they) were Ann Kennedy . . .

PRACTICE WITH *IF . . . WOULD:* GIVING ADVICE

Use the verbs below to tell what you would or wouldn't do if you were Ann Kennedy. Do not use the same verb more than one time.

ask   get   give up   **have**   **speak**   spend   translate

Examples
If I were Ann Kennedy,
a. I _*would speak*_ only Japanese in Japan.
b. I _*wouldn't have*_ conversations in English in Japan.

If I were Ann Kennedy,

1. I _____ my students for advice.
2. I _____ trying to learn Japanese.

3. I _____ frustrated so easily.

4. I _____ more than three months in Japan.

5. I _____ from Japanese to English so much.

Give more advice to Ann Kennedy. Write two of your own complete sentences.

Examples

c. *If I were Ann Kennedy, I would watch Japanese TV.*
d. *If I were Ann Kennedy, I wouldn't worry so much.*

6. _____

7. _____

Vocabulary

Write the appropriate verbs in the spaces provided. Do not use the same verb more than one time. Write the correct tense of the verb that is needed.

admit	feel like	register
attend	form	surround
embarrass	give up	**teach**
express	plan	translate
fascinate	prevent	try

Example

a. That instructor *teaches* very well. His students always learn a lot.

1. My friend doesn't understand a word of English. I always have to _____ everything for her into Spanish.

2. He is _____ very hard to learn English. He studies every day and practices conversation whenever he can.

3. She _____ to visit Europe on her vacation next year.

4. Before you take an English class, you first have to _____ and pay your tuition.

5. My brother _____ me when he laughs at my bad English pronunciation.

6. My friends and I _____ a concert every weekend.

7. Your country really _____ me. It is very beautiful, and the way of life is so interesting and unique.

8. I've tried and tried, but I can't find the answer to this question. I _____. Will you please tell me the answer?

9. I _____ a fool when I make mistakes in Spanish. It really embarrasses me!

10. It is sometimes difficult to _____ your ideas when you write in a foreign language.

11. Beautiful trees and flowers _____ the university on all sides.

12. Students sometimes find it difficult to _____ questions in English.

13. He _____ that he told us a lie yesterday. He said he was sorry, and he told us the truth today.

14. To _____ misunderstandings in a foreign language, always listen carefully and ask questions.

Now supply the appropriate noun.

accent	home	personality	trip
advice	job	pronunciation	trouble
fear	**month**		

Example

b. A *month* usually has thirty or thirty-one days.

15. He's taking a _____ to Rome for his vacation.

16. Some students have _____ speaking English because they find the _____ of English words difficult.

17. After class, she usually goes _____ to eat dinner with her family.

18. I asked my friend to help me with my problem, and she gave me some _____.

19. He has a lot of _____ about speaking a foreign language. He's afraid that other people won't understand him.

20. Most adults who learn a second language speak it with a foreign _____.

21. He makes a lot of money at his new _____. He gets a very good salary.

22. Everyone likes the new student very much. She has a very friendly and charming _____.

Now supply the appropriate adjective.

clever	disappointed	frustrated	helpful
comfortable	envious	glad	kind
deaf	**foreign**	hard	real

Example

c. It's very interesting to visit *foreign* countries. You can learn a lot about other people and their cultures.

23. The students are so _____ they're going on vacation next week. Everyone is happy to have a rest.

24. At first, I felt nervous about living in this new country. But now I feel relaxed and _____ here.

25. I would like to take a trip, but I don't have time now. I feel _____ of people who have enough time to travel.

26. The lesson wasn't easy yesterday. The students found it very _____.

27. The students expected to have a vacation next week. They felt very _____ when they learned it was cancelled.

28. Sometimes I try so hard to pronounce English words, and I feel very _____ when I can't do it!

29. A _____ person doesn't have the ability to hear.

30. She always says something nice to everyone. She is a very _____ person.

31. He's very smart and witty. He always has something _____ to say.

32. Your explanation was very _____ to me. I understand the grammar much better now.

33. That is a _____ diamond necklace, not an artificial one. I'm sure it cost a fortune!

Now supply the appropriate preposition. You may use the same word more than one time.

      about   for   **in**   into   of   to

Example
d. He likes to have conversations __*in*__ English.

34. He spent _____ three or four years _____ the United States.

35. She can translate French _____ English easily because she knows both languages so well.

36. It's hard _____ me to write _____ a foreign language.

37. He never speaks English outside _____ class.

38. I have to admit that I made a lot _____ mistakes.

39. The teacher walked _____ the classroom.

40. His letter is _____ his trip to Japan.

41. Josh can have conversations _____ five different languages because he's spent a lot _____ time _____ different countries. Do you think he dreams _____ five languages, too?

Dictation/Cloze

Listen as your teacher reads, and write the words that you hear in the blank spaces.

Ann Kennedy is _____ 1 _____ 2 teacher who has

_____ 3 learning a _____ 4 language. She is always

_____ 5 to see her students make progress, but sometimes she feels

a little _____ 6 _____ 7 them, too. Ann _____ 8

_____ 9 so happy if she _____ 10 a foreign language. But it's

_____ 11 _____ 12 her to learn one. Ann is very _____ 13 in

the Japanese language. The language and culture of Japan _____ 14

her. She _____ 15 _____ 16 so proud of herself if she

_____ 17 Japanese. She _____ 18 _____ 19 the language

as often as she could. She _____ 20 _____ 21 to her Japanese

friends in Japanese all the time if she _____ 22 more confidence in

her ability to communicate in the language. She _____ 23

_____ 24 conversations with her Japanese students after class if she

_____ 25 the language better. She _____ 26 _____ 27

her favorite Japanese novels in their original language if she _____ 28

more about Japanese grammar and vocabulary.

Next summer, Ann Kennedy is going to Japan. Perhaps if she _____ 29

an effort, she _____ succeed in learning more of the language that

30

_____ her so much.

31

Reading Comprehension

Circle the letter of the correct answers to the following questions.

1. The main idea of this reading passage is:
   a. English teachers can't learn new languages.
   b. An English teacher has difficulties learning a foreign language.
   c. An English teacher takes a trip to Japan.
   d. Japanese is a very difficult language to learn.

2. A detail of this reading passage is:
   a. Ann Kennedy taught English in Japan.
   b. Ann Kennedy attended a Japanese class every evening.
   c. Ann Kennedy made a lot of jokes in Japanese.
   d. Ann Kennedy had trouble understanding spoken Japanese.

3. According to the reading passage, which of the following sentences is true?
   a. Ann Kennedy studied Japanese for several years at the university.
   b. Ann Kennedy didn't want her students to make progress in English.
   c. Ann Kennedy had difficulty forming questions in Japanese, but could usually understand what people said to her.
   d. Words in foreign languages didn't feel real to Ann Kennedy.

4. According to the reading passage, which of the following sentences is *not* true?
   a. Ann Kennedy visited Japan once.
   b. Ann thought her Japanese pronunciation was good.
   c. Ann was afraid of making mistakes in Japanese.
   d. Ann's Japanese friends in Japan spoke English.

5. In your opinion, based on the reading passage, which of the following sentences is true?
   a. Ann Kennedy probably plans to marry a Japanese man.
   b. Ann Kennedy probably enjoys teaching foreign students because she is interested in other languages and cultures.
   c. Ann feels very confident in her ability to learn a foreign language.
   d. It's difficult for Ann to learn Japanese, but she probably speaks other foreign languages well.

6. Which pair has the words that are most similar in meaning?
   a. *envious* and *jealous*
   b. *confused* and *frustrated*
   c. *comfortable* and *carefully*
   d. *glad* and *kind*

Guessing Meanings from Context

Guess the meanings of the italicized words from the context. Circle the letter of the word or words that are most similar in meaning to the italicized word(s):

> **Example**
>
> English spelling can be difficult. Even native speakers of English make *errors* in spelling sometimes.
> **ⓐ** mistakes
> **b.** problems
> **c.** erase
> **d.** words

1. Many people feel a lot of *anxiety* about speaking a foreign language because they are afraid of making mistakes.
   a. angry
   b. variety
   c. difficult
   d. nervousness

2. After living in Italy for many years, he spoke *fluent* Italian.
   a. a long time
   b. fast
   c. easy, without effort
   d. good pronunciation

3. A good teacher *encourages* students to learn new things.
   a. feels envious
   b. is strict
   c. gives hope and confidence
   d. insists

4. His poor listening comprehension *discouraged* him from practicing his English conversation. Finally, he gave up speaking English.
   a. prevented
   b. took away hope and confidence

   c. made him brave
   d. destroyed

5. Ann Kennedy *signed up* for a Japanese class as soon as she arrived in Japan.
   a. attended
   b. sat in
   c. wrote
   d. registered

6. If you live in a foreign country for a while, you will usually *pick up* some of the language even without taking a class.
   a. learn from formal instruction
   b. learn from textbooks
   c. learn just by having contact with the language
   d. fail to learn

7. We have to *pick up* our friend at the airport.
   a. opposite of "drop off"
   b. choose
   c. drive
   d. opposite of "put down"

8. I *envy* people who travel a lot. I don't have much opportunity to travel.
   a. am angry
   b. feel jealous of
   c. enjoy
   d. take many trips

Word Forms: What Is an Adverb?

We know that an *adjective* is a word that describes a *noun*. For example, if we say, "He is a nervous person," the word *nervous* (adjective) describes what kind of *person* (noun) he is.

An *adverb* is a word that describes a *verb*. For example, if we say, "He speaks nervously," the word *nervously* (adverb) describes how he speaks (verb). We usually form an adverb by adding *-ly* to an adjective: nervous— nervously.

Below are more examples of adjectives and their corresponding adverbs:

careful   carefully
comfortable   comfortably

fluent	fluently
glad	gladly
kind	kindly
quick	quickly
slow	slowly

Decide which form of the word is needed in the sentences below:

Example

careful, carefully

He is a *careful*_____ student. He always does his work

*carefully*_____ .

1. **comfortable, comfortably**

This is a very _____ bed. I slept _____ all night.

2. **fluent, fluently**

He is a _____ speaker of Spanish. He speaks the language

_____ .

3. **kind, kindly**

Please speak _____ to her. She's very depressed, and a few

_____ words will help her.

4. **glad, gladly**

He smiled _____ when he saw his girlfriend. His girlfriend

had a _____ smile for him, too.

5. **quick, quickly**

Rabbits are _____ animals. They run _____ all the

time.

6. **slow, slowly**

We are taking the _____ boat. We'll cross the river

_____ .

Group Activities

SMALL GROUP RETELLING OF STORY AND DISCUSSION

Work with a small group of students. Each student in the group can retell a little of the story of Ann Kennedy until the entire story has been retold. After that, each student can give his or her opinion of the story, and advice to Ann Kennedy. If you were Ann, what would you do on your next trip to Japan to make the language learning experience more successful?

Also, discuss the following questions with members of your group: Do you have some of the same problems that Ann Kennedy has learning foreign languages? Is it difficult for you to understand English sometimes? Do you have to translate from English to your native language when you speak, write, or read? Is it easy for you to pronounce English words? Do you sometimes feel nervous or embarrassed when you speak English? Do you always understand what other people say to you? Do other people always understand what you say to them in English? What other problems do you have in English?

ROLE-PLAYS

Divide the class into small groups or pairs. Each group or pair can choose one of the following situations:

1. Ann Kennedy tells you (and perhaps some other students, too) her problems with learning foreign languages, and asks you for advice. You give her advice and try to encourage her. Write some lines of dialogue to role-play for the rest of the class.

2. Imagine that Ann Kennedy has returned from her second trip to Japan. This time, she has learned a lot more Japanese. She is very happy and excited. You ask her why she was more successful this time. She explains. Write some lines of dialogue to role-play for the rest of the class.

3. You go into a store and ask the clerk for something. The clerk doesn't understand your English. You have to repeat your words many times before the clerk finally understands what you want. Write some lines of dialogue to role-play for the rest of the class.

SIMON SAYS

Listen as your teacher tells you to act out the various emotions and actions mentioned in this chapter and previous chapters. Act out the emotions and actions only if your teacher first says the words *Simon says*. If you make a mistake, you must sit down and stop playing the game. The last person left standing is the winner.

Possible commands are:

Look nervous.	Look interested.
Look frustrated.	Look fascinated.
Look confused.	Look afraid.
Look comfortable.	Look disappointed.
Look envious.	Think carefully.

AN INTERVIEW WITH THE TEACHER

Ask your teacher about his or her experiences learning a foreign language. Does your teacher speak one or more foreign languages? If not, is he or she interested in learning one? What are some difficulties your teacher has in foreign language learning?

SITUATION 1

SITUATION 2

SITUATION 3

SITUATION 4

SITUATION 5

chapter 12

Social Mistakes Across Cultures

The Unreal Conditional: If . . . Would

Pre-reading Questions

Is the social life in the United States the same as the social life in your country?

Do people always arrive on time to parties, dinners, classes, and business appointments in your country? In the United States?

Do you always telephone a friend before you visit him or her in your country? In the United States?

Did you ever feel confused or unsure about the customs or social rules in a foreign country?

Read (and listen) to each story. Look at the pictures and tell what you see.

Social Mistakes Across Cultures

Situation 1

It is 7:30 on a Thursday evening.[1] Laura and Dan, a young American couple, are having dinner together and relaxing after a long, hard day—and week—of work. They are enjoying the chance to spend some time alone together.[2] Suddenly the doorbell rings.[3] Laura and Dan are surprised because they are not expecting any company.[4] Laura answers the door and finds her friend Maria from the university.[5] Maria is from the Dominican Republic. She came to the United States just several months ago.[6] "Hi," says Maria happily. "I thought it would be nice if we could spend the evening together."[7] But is is clear to Maria that Laura and Dan are not really glad to see her.[8] "Sure," Laura says. "Come in and sit down." But Laura does not smile and is not enthusiastic.[9] Maria feels that she has made some mistake, but she doesn't know what it is.[10]

What mistake did Maria make? What is the problem here? What would you do if you were in this situation? What would you do if you were Maria? What would you do if you were Laura or Dan?

1. What is the day and time?
2. Who are Laura and Dan? What are they doing?
3. What happens suddenly?
4. How do Laura and Dan feel?
5. Who is at the door?
6. Where is Maria from? Did she come to the United States a long time ago?
7. What does Maria say?
8. What is clear to Maria?
9. How does Laura feel about Maria's visit?
10. How does Maria feel?

Situation 2

Kate and George, an American couple, have invited their friends Teresa and Fernando to come over and visit for the evening.[1] Teresa and Fernando are from Brazil.[2] They moved to the United States several months ago, and are glad they have finally met some American friends.[3] Kate and George are expecting Teresa and Fernando to arrive at 7:00 P.M.[4] They have prepared a table with a bottle of wine and some glasses, and also some cheese and crackers.[5] They wait for their friends to come. But at 7:30, Teresa and Fernando have still not appeared.[6] At

8:30, they have *still* not appeared.[7] Finally, they arrive at 9:00 P.M.[8] By this time, Kate and George have put away the refreshments because they assumed their friends were not coming.[9] They expect some explanation from Teresa and Fernando about why they are so late.[10] But they receive no explanation.[11] They feel a bit annoyed with Teresa and Fernando.[12]

What is the problem here? Why are Kate and George annoyed? Why don't Teresa and Fernando explain why they are late? What would you do if you were the American couple? What would you do if you were the Brazilian couple?

1. Who are Kate and George? Whom did they invite to visit for the evening?
2. Where are Teresa and Fernando from?
3. When did they move to the United States? What are they happy about?
4. When are Kate and George expecting their friends to arrive?
5. What did Kate and George do?
6. What happens at 7:30?
7. What happens at 8:30?
8. What happens at 9:00 P.M.?
9. What did Kate and George do? Why?
10. What do Kate and George expect?
11. What do they receive?
12. How do Kate and George feel?

Situation 3

Don and Paula, two American tourists, are walking along a street in a small village in China.[1] They have their arms around each other and are in a very romantic mood.[2] Suddenly, they stop and begin to kiss each other passionately.[3] When they stop, they notice that several of the village people are exchanging very disapproving glances with each other.[4]

What is the problem here? Why are the village people exchanging disapproving glances? What would you do if you were in this situation?

1. Who are Don and Paula? What are they doing?
2. Where are their arms? What kind of mood are they in?
3. What do they suddenly do?
4. What do they notice when they stop?

Situation 4

Sako, a Japanese student, and Maxine, an American student, are friends.[1] On her birthday, Maxine receives a present from Sako.[2] She accepts the gift very enthusiastically. "Oh, how nice of you, Sako!" Maxine says.[3] Maxine then opens Sako's gift.[4] It is a Japanese kite.[5] "Oh, what a wonderful gift!" says Maxine excitedly. "I love it!"[6] At this point, Maxine notices that Sako looks very embarrassed and uncomfortable.[7] Maxine thinks that perhaps Sako doesn't believe that she really likes the gift.[8] "I really mean it!" Maxine tells Sako. "It's the most adorable gift! I'm crazy about it!"[9] But Sako looks even more uncomfortable after Maxine tries to reassure her.[10]

What is the problem here? Why is Sako uncomfortable? What would you do if you were in this situation?

1. Who are Sako and Maxine?
2. What happens on Maxine's birthday?
3. How does Maxine accept Sako's gift? What does she say?
4. What does Maxine do?
5. What is the gift?
6. What does Maxine say?
7. What does Maxine notice?
8. What does Maxine think?
9. What does Maxine tell Sako?
10. How does Sako look after Maxine tries to reassure her?

Situation 5

Tahir, a Turkish student, invites Chrissy and Sean, two American students, to his home for dinner.[1] He prepares a Turkish meal for them.[2] They enjoy the dinner very much, and tell Tahir how much they like it.[3]

"Have some more," Tahir says, and begins to fill their plates.[4]

"Oh no thanks, Tahir," says Sean. "It was delicious, but we're really full."

"Yes, we loved it, but we're stuffed," Chrissy tells him.[5]

"You mean you don't like my food? You must eat more!" Tahir insists. "And you must drink some more wine, too!"[6]

"The food was great," answers Sean. "But we really can't handle another bite."[7]

"And we shouldn't drink any more wine," Chrissy adds. "We have to get up for class tomorrow."[8]

"If you don't drink more of my wine and eat more of my food, you'll insult me," says Tahir.[9]

Chrissy and Sean exchange exasperated glances.[10] They are really not hungry anymore.[11] They pick at their food.[12]

As the evening goes on, Tahir continues to offer more food and wine and to fill the plates and glasses of his guests. Chrissy and Sean become quieter and quieter.[13] Finally, they tell Tahir that they must go home.[14] Tahir invites Chrissy and Sean to come for dinner again the following week.[15]

"We'll be pretty busy next week," Sean says.[16]

"Of course you'll have dinner with me next week," says Tahir. "I'll see you next Thursday night."[17]

"Well—maybe," Chrissy tells him, and looks away.[18]

Tahir feels that something is wrong. Chrissy and Sean are distant and silent, and he doesn't understand why.[19] Tahir believes that he was a good, generous host.[20]

What is the problem here? Why do Chrissy and Sean become distant and silent? What would you do if you were Tahir? What would you do if you were Chrissy or Sean?

1. Who is Tahir? What does he do?
2. What does he cook for his American friends?
3. Do Chrissy and Sean like the dinner? Do they tell Tahir?
4. What does Tahir say? What does he do?
5. How do Chrissy and Sean feel? What do they say to Tahir?
6. What does Tahir insist?
7. What does Sean answer?
8. What does Chrissy add?
9. What does Tahir say?
10. What do Chrissy and Sean do?
11. How do they feel?
12. Do they eat their food?
13. What happens as the evening goes on?
14. What do Chrissy and Sean finally tell Tahir?
15. What does Tahir do?
16. What does Sean answer?
17. What does Tahir say?
18. What does Chrissy tell him?
19. How does Tahir feel? What does he think of Sean's and Chrissy's conduct?
20. What does Tahir believe?

Vocabulary

Write the appropriate verbs in the spaces provided, using the correct tense of the verb that is needed. Do not use the same verb more than one time.

accept	expect	insult	put away
add	fill	invite	reassure
assume	get up	**move**	relax
come in	go on	offer	ring
come over	handle	pick at	wait for
exchange	have dinner		

Example

a. He **moved** to his new home in the United States three years ago.

1. "I would like to _____ you to my party," he said. "Please come at 8:00."

2. We _____ his invitation and went to the party.

3. "Open the door and _____," she said. "I'm happy you came to visit."

4. "Yes, I would like to see you," she said. "I'll _____ after work and visit."

5. In the United States, we usually don't _____ food to guests more than once or twice.

6. The telephone _____. Will you answer it?

7. On our vacation, we didn't want to work. We wanted to _____.

8. We usually _____ at 8:00. We are all hungry by that time.

9. You never eat any of the desserts that I make, so I _____ that you don't like them.

10. I would like to call you some time. I want you to call me, too. Can we _____ telephone numbers?

11. I don't think he's hungry. He's not eating his lunch. He's just
    _____ it.

12. "Please _____ the dishes after you finish washing and dry-
    ing them," she told us.

13. Everyone wants more coffee. Please _____ everybody's cup
    again.

14. Sometimes we have to _____ the bus for more than twenty
    minutes.

15. I'm angry because he said that I was stupid and lazy. He
    _____ me!

16. She didn't believe that we liked the dinner she cooked. We had to
    _____ her many times that it was delicious.

17. In the United States, people usually _____ their guests to
    telephone if they are going to be late.

18. The party _____ for a long time. It ended at three o'clock in
    the morning.

19. Ten guests will sit at the dinner table. If we _____ three
    more, there will be thirteen. That's an unlucky number!

20. When my alarm clock rings at seven o'clock in the morning, I
    _____ and get ready for work.

21. He can't _____ his problem alone. He needs someone to
    help him.

Now supply the appropriate noun.

chance	doorbell	glance	mood
company	**evening**	host	refreshments
cracker	gift	kite	village

Example

    b. Our friends arrived at our home at two o'clock in the after-
noon, and left at seven o'clock in the _**evening**_.

22. In many countries, it is usual for people to receive _____ on
    their birthdays.

23. The _____ is ringing. It's probably my friend Jim coming to visit.

24. He's not accustomed to life in a big city. He comes from a small _____.

25. For _____, there are _____, cheese, sandwiches, and soft drinks.

26. He didn't smile once all day. I think he's in a bad _____.

27. He moved his eyes and gave a _____ in the attractive woman's direction. Then he quickly looked away.

28. A good _____ tries to make all the guests happy and comfortable.

29. The _____ is going to arrive at 7:00. We are making dinner for them.

30. Now that he has some American friends, he has the _____ to practice his English often.

31. The children are flying their new _____ in the park.

Now supply the appropriate adjective.

adorable	crazy	enthusiastic	romantic
alone	disapproving	exasperated	rude
annoyed	distant	generous	silent
clear	embarrassed	glad	uncomfortable

Example

c. After the guests left the party, the host was *alone* _____ in his home.

32. "Please stop talking," the teacher said to the students. "Be _____ and listen carefully."

33. In some cultures, it's _____ not to accept food that is offered to you.

34. The boyfriend and girlfriend enjoyed dancing to _____ music.

35. Her face always gets red when she is _____.

36. The host was very _____ that all the guests liked his party so much.

37. In most countries, people feel _____ about parties and other social events.

38. His parents are very _____ on his birthday. They give him lots of gifts and money.

39. Sometimes we feel _____ living in a new country when we are not accustomed to its way of life.

40. In some cultures, there is a _____ attitude toward public affection because the customs don't permit it.

41. It can be difficult to feel close to people when they are angry. They often become very _____ from us psychologically.

42. The teacher was very _____ when so many students arrived to class late.

43. What an _____ child! She's just lovely!

44. I'm _____ about ice cream! I could eat it all day long!

45. It's very _____ that he's in a good mood today. Everyone can see that he can't stop smiling.

46. The host felt _____ with two of the guests who always arrived late for dinner parties.

Now supply the appropriate adverb.

enthusiastically	**happily**	recently
excitedly	passionately	suddenly

Example

d. She has a very happy smile whenever she sees her boyfriend.
   She always smiles _*happily*_ at him.

47. He was very enthusiastic about the delicious meal you cooked last night. He talked about it very _____.

48. "I'm very excited about meeting people in your country," she said. "It will be so interesting to get to know them!" she said

_____.

49. He made a recent trip to the United States. He visited there

_____.

50. No one expected his sudden anger. He became angry very

_____.

51. They have a passionate love for each other. They love each other

_____.

Now supply the appropriate preposition. You can use the same word more than one time.

about   **for**   in   to
along   from   on   with
at

Example

e. "Please come over _**for**_ dinner soon," he said to us.

52. We're arriving _____ Wednesday afternoon _____ 2:00 P.M.
53. I love to walk _____ the beautiful streets of Paris.
54. Our party is _____ seven o'clock _____ midnight.
55. He's always _____ a good mood _____ Friday because he loves the weekend.
56. She is annoyed _____ her husband because he forgot to buy her a birthday gift.
57. We can't wait _____ him any longer. We're already late.
58. I'm so glad to see you. We haven't seen each other _____ several months.
59. In almost every country, it's important to get to class _____ time.

Dictation/Cloze

Listen as your teacher reads, and write the words that you hear in the blank spaces.

Every culture _____ different rules _____ commu-
                        1   2
nication _____ social situations. If you _____ in a differ-
                  3   4
ent country for a while, you _____ _____ new rules and
                                      5   6
customs. For example, if you _____ time in South America, you
                                         7
_____ _____ to view time differently. You _____
        8   9   10
often _____ later for social events than you _____ in
              11   12
North America, for example.

If you _____ in Japan for a time, perhaps you _____
                13   14
_____ gifts in a different manner. You _____
          15   16
_____ them immediately and you _____ _____
        17   18   19
them excessively.

If you _____ to the United States, you _____
                20   21
_____ accustomed to calling friends on the telephone before visit-
        22
ing them. At an American dinner party, you _____ _____
                                                    23   24
a guest food more than one or two times. You _____ _____
                                                        25   26
his or her refusal.

So, if you _____ to a new country, you _____
                    27   28
_____ to learn two new languages: the spoken language of words,
        29
and the unspoken language of social interaction.

Reading Comprehension

Circle the letter of the correct answers to the following questions.

1. The main idea of these reading passages is:
   a. People make social mistakes when they don't know the social rules of another culture.
   b. People from many countries around the world are impolite.
   c. Every culture has the same social rules.
   d. Americans like everyone to arrive on time.

2. A detail of Situation 2 is:
   a. Teresa and Fernando are rude people.
   b. Teresa and Fernando have many American friends.
   c. The American couple is a little angry when they receive no explanation for the Brazilian couple's lateness.
   d. American people and Brazilian people have different ideas about time.

3. Which of the following sentences is true according to the reading passages?
   a. Kate and George have prepared dinner for their guests.
   b. Maxine doesn't really like the gift she received from Sako.
   c. Sean and Chrissy don't like Turkish food.
   d. Teresa and Fernando arrived at Kate and George's home two hours late.

4. According to the reading passages, which of the following sentences is *not* true?
   a. Laura and Dan are surprised when the doorbell rings.
   b. Kate and George have prepared some snacks for their guests.
   c. The village people in China look at each other and smile when they see the American couple kissing on the street.
   d. Tahir offers his American friends food many times, and is very insistent that they accept it.

5. In your opinion, based on the reading passages, which of the following sentences is true?
   a. Maxine is trying to embarrass Sako.
   b. People in small villages in China are not accustomed to public displays of affection.
   c. Chrissy and Sean really want more food, but they think it's polite to refuse Tahir's offer.
   d. Teresa and Fernando don't explain their lateness because they are embarrassed.

6. Which pair has the words that are most similar in meaning?
   a. *exchange* and *examine*
   b. *refreshments* and *dinner*
   c. *reassure* and *tell a lie*
   d. *annoyed* and *angry*

Guessing Meanings from Context

Guess the meanings of the italicized words from the context. Circle the letter of the word or words that are most similar in meaning to the italicized word(s):

Example

It was a big party! The host invited more than one hundred *guests!*
a. invitations
b. people who give a party
ⓒ people who come to a party
d. people who clean up after a party

1. She received a lot of *praise* for the wonderful dinner she made. Everyone said it was absolutely delicious.
   a. compliments; kind words
   b. money and gifts
   c. dishes
   d. please

2. He *refused* our invitation to lunch because he had other plans.
   a. accepted
   b. didn't accept
   c. accepted again
   d. didn't like

3. Mr. Otis and his wife are the host and *hostess* of the party.
   a. woman who comes to a party
   b. man who comes to a party
   c. man who gives a party
   d. woman who gives a party

4. Every culture has certain *rules* for different social situations.
   a. rights
   b. kinds of conduct that are impolite
   c. rude
   d. "laws" or regulations for conduct

5. If we don't know the social rules of a culture, we can find ourselves in some *awkward* situations.
   a. embarrassing
   b. forward
   c. interesting
   d. impolite

6. In the United States, many people go to work on *weekdays* and see their friends on weekends.
   a. Monday through Friday
   b. Saturday and Sunday
   c. weeks and days
   d. Monday through Sunday

7. The party began at 7:00 P.M., but most of the guests didn't *show up* until 8:00 or 9:00.
   a. display
   b. late
   c. appear
   d. shower

8. We spent a long time *getting ready* for our guests. We cleaned the house and cooked all day.
   a. being polite
   b. making food
   c. working
   d. preparing

Word Forms

Generally, the prefix *re-* means *again*. If we put the letters *re-* in front of a word, it adds the meaning *again*. For example, the word *reassure* means *assure again*. The word *retell* means *tell again*.

Below are some common words with the prefix *re-*. Rewrite the following sentences using the words below:

rebuild   remake   review   **retell**
relive   reunite   rewrite

Example

The child asked his mother to tell the story again.

The child asked his mother to retell the story.

1. The teacher asked the students to write their compositions again.

   _____

2. I'd like to live the happiest day of my life again.

   _____

3. After the Civil War, the northern and southern states of the United States united again.

   _____

4. The film director wants to make that old movie again.

_____

5. They're going to build the old church again.

_____

Group Activities

SMALL GROUP RETELLING OF STORY AND DISCUSSION

Work with a small group of students. Each student in the group can retell a little of each of the "Situations" until all of them have been retold. After that, each student can tell what he or she would do if he or she were in that situation. For example, what would you do if you were Maria? What would you do if you were Laura or Dan, Kate or George? And so on.

Also, discuss the following questions with the members of your group: Did you ever have an uncomfortable experience in the United States or another country because you didn't know the social rules of that culture? What are some things about the social life and customs of the United States or other countries that you don't understand? What things confuse you? What can people do to understand other cultures better?

ROLE-PLAYS

Divide the class into small groups or pairs. Each group or pair can choose one of the "Situations" to act out for the rest of the class. Also, show what happens *next* in the situation. What do the people say? What do they do? Write at least six-to-eight lines of dialogue.

SIMON SAYS

Listen as your teacher tells you to act out the various emotions and actions mentioned in this chapter and previous chapters. Act out the emotions and actions only if your teacher first says the words *Simon says*. If you make a mistake, you must sit down and stop playing the game. The last person left standing is the winner.

Possible commands are:

Look surprised.	Look enthusiastic.
Look annoyed.	Fill a glass with wine.
Look embarrassed.	Drink the wine.
Look insulted.	Pour some more wine.
Look relaxed.	Drink some more wine.
Look uncomfortable.	Spill some wine.

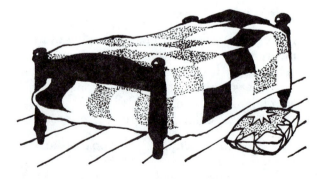

chapter 13

The Amish People and the Pennsylvania Dutch Country

Present Perfect Progressive

Pre-reading Questions

Look at the pictures. What do you see?
Do you think the people in the pictures are living in the twentieth century?
Why or why not?

The Amish People and the Pennsylvania Dutch Country

In such a technologically advanced country as the United States, who would believe there is a place where people choose to live without electricity, running water, automobiles, and other modern conveniences? Who would believe there is a place where people still live and dress as they did almost three hundred years ago?

Among the *Pennsylvania Dutch* of Lancaster County, Pennsylvania, there is a community of people known as the *Amish*. The Amish people have been living in the same traditional way since their German ancestors first settled in the United States in 1727.[1] The Amish are members of a Christian sect founded in 1693 by Jacob Amman of Switzerland. Jacob Amman believed that Christians should live plain and simple lives. He believed that Christians should not fill their lives with "worldly" things. Amman didn't think that Christians should conform to the materialism, vanity, or complexity of the larger society.[2] So the followers of Jacob Amman have been avoiding the increasing modernization of life for the last two and a half centuries. They have been driving the same simple horse-drawn wagons for over two hundred and fifty years. They haven't been using cars or other modern vehicles. They've been unwilling to use any mechanical appliances. They've been farming in the same way since they first settled in the United States. The Amish farmers have been using horses to work the land instead of tractors and other mechanical farm equipment. They've been building their own houses and furniture by hand without the aid of machinery.[3]

Many members of the Pennsylvania Dutch community have always been superstitious.[4] They've been protecting their homes, land, and animals with special *hex signs* for centuries. They've been hanging these hex signs on their houses and barns to keep away evil spirits[5] so their lives can remain peaceful and simple.

Amish women like to dress very simply. They have never been interested in fashionable clothing or cosmetics.[6] They've been wearing the same very simple, long, dark dresses and bonnets for almost three hundred years.[7] The Amish men have been wearing the same simple, dark shirts and jackets, pants with suspenders, broad-brimmed hats, and long beards for several hundred years.[8]

The men and women of the Amish country have a language of their own, too. They have been speaking their Pennsylvania Dutch dialect for many, many years.[9] This dialect has been changing, however. Over the years, more and more English words have been entering the language of the Pennsylvania Dutch. Now, their dialect is often a combination of German grammatical structures and English vocabulary.[10]

Like all other cultures, the Pennsylvania Dutch community has its own special kind of cooking as well. A Pennsylvania Dutch term that many Americans know is *shoofly pie*.[11] Shoofly pie is one of the delicious desserts that the Pennsylvania Dutch have been making for a couple of centuries. It's made with molasses and sweet-dough crumbs, and is a great favorite among tourists who visit Pennsylvania Dutch country.[12] The food of this community is very hearty and delicious.[13] These people have been cooking tasty food in their simple wood-burning stoves for the last few hundred years.[14] Other famous dishes are Pennsylvania Dutch dumplings, noodles, and apple butter.[15]

In addition to making wonderful food, the Pennsylvania Dutch have been making their own handicrafts for years and years.[16] They have been designing and sewing beautiful quilts and pillows since their settlement first began.[17]

If you are in the United States, you can visit the Amish community in Lancaster, Pennsylvania.[18] You can see the homes of the Amish people, buy their handicrafts in shops, and taste Pennsylvania Dutch cooking.[19]

There are also communities of Amish people in other parts of the United States. You can find them in Holmes County, Ohio, and Elkhart County, Indiana.[20]

In such a culturally diverse country as the United States, you can find all kinds of surprising places and people.[21]

1. What community can we find in Lancaster County, Pennsylvania? How have they been living since 1727?
2. What religion are the Amish people? Who was Jacob Amman? What did he believe?
3. What have the followers of Jacob Amman been doing?
4. Are the Pennsylvania Dutch people superstitious?
5. What have they been doing for centuries?
6. Have the Amish women always been interested in fashionable clothing and cosmetics?
7. What kind of clothes have they been wearing for almost three hundred years?
8. What kind of clothes have the Amish men been wearing for almost three hundred years?
9. What language do the Amish people speak?
10. Has the language of the Pennsylvania Dutch been changing over the years? How?
11. What Pennsylvania Dutch term do many Americans know?
12. What is shoofly pie?
13. Describe Pennsylvania Dutch food.
14. What have the Amish people been using to cook their food for the last few hundred years?
15. What are some other famous Pennsylvania Dutch dishes?
16. What have the Amish women been making in addition to wonderful food?
17. What kinds of things have they been making?
18. Where can you visit if you are in the United States?
19. What can you do there?

20. Where else can you find Amish communities?
21. What kind of country is the United States? What can you find in it?

The Present Perfect Progressive

We use the present perfect progressive tense to describe an action that began in the past and has been continuing until the present time. We may also expect the action to continue into the future:

subject	present tense *have*	been	verb + -ing	(time)
The Amish people	have	been	farming	for years.
That Amish woman	has	been	cooking	since 4:00.

To form a question, we reverse the position of the subject and *have*:

present tense *have*	subject	been	verb + -ing	(time)
Have	the Amish people	been	farming	for years?
Has	that Amish woman	been	cooking	since 4:00?

To form a negative sentence, we put *not* after *have*:

subject	present tense *have*	*not* been verb + -ing	(time)
The Amish people	have	not been farming	for years.
That Amish woman	has	not been cooking	since 4:00.

We can put *have* and *not* together to form the following contractions:

have + not = haven't
has + not = hasn't

Vocabulary

Write the appropriate verbs in the spaces provided. Do not use the same verb more than one time. Use the correct tense of the verb that is needed.

avoid	conform	follow	settle
be founded	design	hang	sew
build	farm	protect	taste
choose			

Example

a. There are so many beautiful quilts in this shop that it's difficult to **Choose** just one.

1. This shoofly pie _____ delicious! I'd like another piece.

2. We like to _____ photographs of all our trips on the wall.

3. He doesn't really want to work. He always finds a reason to
_____ looking for a job.

4. We've been _____ this land for many years. We grow fruits,
vegetables, and flowers.

5. People from many parts of the world left their native countries to
_____ in the United States.

6. Many people left their native countries and came to the United States
because they didn't want to _____ to the rules and conduct
of their own societies.

7. Before you _____ a house, you first have to _____ it.

8. She never buys clothes because she _____ them all herself.

9. She's wearing sunglasses to _____ her eyes from the strong
sun.

10. It's generally important for students to _____ the instructions of the teacher.

11. The United States of America _____ officially
_____ in 1776.

Now supply the appropriate noun.

aid	convenience	hex	sect
appliance	cosmetics	horse-drawn	settlement
barn	crumb	wagon	sign
beard	dialect	materialism	**stove**
bonnet	dough	modernization	suspenders
broad brimmed	dumpling	molasses	tractor
hat	electricity	pillow	vanity
combination	equipment	quilt	vehicle
complexity	handicraft		

Example

b. The Amish people cook their food on wood-burning
**stoves** .

12. If we want to bake bread, we must first mix some _____.

13. _____ are a food that has dough on the outside, and meat, vegetables, or fruit on the inside.

14. _____ is a sweet syrup that comes from sugar.

15. In the winter, when the weather is cold, people often sleep with heavy _____ on their beds to keep warm.

16. Most people sleep on beds with _____ under their heads.

17. Articles of sewing, knitting, and other handmade things are examples of _____.

18. In many countries, women like to wear lipstick and other _____ on their faces to look more attractive.

19. Many years ago, a lot of women wore large hats called _____.

20. Like the Amish men, cowboys also wear _____.

21. A _____ is a building on a farm where cows, chickens, and other animals live.

22. The old woman is feeding some _____ of bread to the birds.

23. Irons and toasters are _____ that are commonly found in homes in many different countries.

24. Washing machines, vacuum cleaners, and other modern _____ make housework faster and easier.

25. Before the invention of the automobile, many people drove _____.

26. The _____ of life in this century has been the result of advances in technology.

27. There is often a lot of _____ in modern societies. People are interested in making more and more money, and buying and owning more and more things.

28. Modern farmers use _____ instead of animals to work their land.

29. Before men commonly wore belts, they wore _____ with their pants.

30. Buses, trains, and airplanes are examples of modern _____.

31. Modern life isn't simple. There is a lot of _____ in today's world.

32. We stopped our car when we saw the "stop _____" on the road.

33. People from Europe formed the first _____ in the United States.

34. The Amish people are a _____ of Christianity. They disagree with the way many Christians practice the religion.

35. Usually, one language has different _____; the vocabulary and grammar can vary, depending on where it is spoken.

36. Amish men wear long _____ on their faces.

37. In some societies, some people seem to think that an attractive appearance is more important than a good character. There is a lot of _____ in these societies.

38. The witch put a _____ on that man. Now he has bad luck all the time.

39. People generally have more free time in modern society, thanks to the _____ of electrical and other modern conveniences.

40. Her mother is German and her father is Italian, so she is a _____ of German and Italian.

41. Baseball bats, golf clubs, and tennis rackets are examples of sports _____.

Now supply the appropriate adjective.

broad	hearty	**modern**	wood-burning
evil	increasing	plain	worldly
famous	mechanical	running	

Example

c. The Amish people want to keep their traditional life-style. They don't want to change to a **modern**____ way of life.

42. Many years ago, people did not have sinks with faucets and _____ water.

43. In modern times, many homes have dishwashers, vacuum cleaners, and other _____ appliances.

44. In American society, _____ numbers of women are working outside the home.

45. _____ is the opposite of good.

46. Florida is _____ for its sunshine and beaches.

47. We have an old-fashioned _____ fireplace in our living room. It makes the room warm and cozy in winter time.

48. When she went to parties, she wore very fancy, elegant clothes. But she always dressed in the opposite way at work. She wore very _____ dresses.

49. Football players rarely have thin, narrow shoulders. They generally have strong, _____ shoulders.

50. He was not interested in having a lot of money, material success, or other _____ things. He was interested in pursuing spiritual things.

51. He doesn't eat a nutritious diet. He could use a _____ meal.

Now supply the appropriate preposition. You may use the same word more than one time.

in   for   of   to   with

Example

d. The Amish people live __*in*__ Lancaster, Pennsylvania.

52. The Amish people have been living _____ the same way _____ several hundred years.

53. The Amish people don't want to conform _____ the modern way _____ life.

54. The Amish don't want to fill their lives _____ worldly things.

55. _____ addition _____ their cooking, the Pennsylvania Dutch are famous _____ their handicrafts.

56. The Amish people are followers _____ Jacob Amman.

Dictation/Cloze

Listen as your teacher reads, and write the words that you hear in the blank spaces.

The Amish people _____ _____ _____ in
₁ ₂ ₃

the same way since they first _____ in Pennsylvania _____
₄ ₅

1727. They _____ _____ _____ the same farm-
₆ ₇ ₈

ing methods and equipment _____ over two centuries. They
₉

_____ _____ _____ horse-drawn wagons in-
₁₀ ₁₁ ₁₂

stead of automobiles and other motor-powered _____. They
₁₃

_____ _____ _____ _____ up with the
₁₄ ₁₅ ₁₆ ₁₇

technology of the _____ world because their religious beliefs
₁₈

_____ this.
₁₉

The Amish people _____ also _____ _____
₂₀ ₂₁ ₂₂

the same style of clothing for many, many years. The typical Amish woman

_____   _____   _____ a _____ style,
23   24   25   26

long, dark dress and bonnet for the last couple of centuries. The typical

Amish man _____   _____   _____ the same style
27   28   29

_____-brimmed hat, simple shirt, and pants _____ sus-
30   31

penders since the earliest settlement in America. The Amish people

_____   _____   _____   _____ the latest
32   33   34   35

fashions.

The food of the Pennsylvania Dutch people is _____ and
36

delicious. They _____   _____   _____ and
37   38   39

_____ their traditional recipes for a great number of years. Tour-
40

ists who visit these communities _____   _____
41   42

_____ and _____ wonderful Pennsylvania Dutch cook-
43   44

ing for many years too.

The Pennsylvania Dutch, and especially the Amish community,

_____   _____   _____ a special and unique way of
45   46   47

life for many years.

Reading Comprehension

Circle the letter of the correct answers to the following questions.

1. The main idea of this reading passage is:
    a. Various kinds of unusual communities exist in the United States.
    b. The Amish community of the Pennsylvania Dutch country has a special way of life.
    c. The Amish people should try to keep up with modern times.
    d. The Amish people don't use modern conveniences.

2. A detail of this reading passage is:
   a. The Amish people don't use modern conveniences.
   b. Many people in the United States are old-fashioned, not just the Amish people.
   c. The Amish people don't speak English correctly.
   d. The Amish women wear broad-brimmed hats and pants with suspenders.

3. Which of the following sentences is true according to the reading passage?
   a. The Amish women are interested in fashionable clothes and make-up.
   b. The Amish women make beautiful pillows and cosmetics.
   c. The Amish men use mechanical farm equipment.
   d. The Amish people have their own Pennsylvania Dutch dialect.

4. Which of the following sentences is *not* true according to the reading passage?
   a. Some of the Pennsylvania Dutch people put up hex signs to protect their homes.
   b. The Pennsylvania Dutch people have been cooking delicious food for the last few hundred years.
   c. The Amish men wear simple, dark clothing and bonnets.
   d. Jacob Amman was from Europe.

5. In your opinion, based on the reading passage, which of the following sentences is true?
   a. Many Americans live like the Amish people.
   b. The Amish people probably enjoy traveling to other countries.
   c. By visiting the Amish people, we can learn about the life-style of many of the earliest settlers in America.
   d. By visiting the Amish people, we can learn something about the life-styles of many Americans in modern society.

6. Which pair has the words that are most similar in meaning?
   a. *language* and *dialect*
   b. *farm* and *land*
   c. *settle* and *inhabit*
   d. *pillow* and *quilt*

Guessing Meanings from Context

Guess the meanings of the italicized words from the context. Circle the letter of the word or words that are most similar in meaning to the italicized word(s):

Example

The Amish people live an *old-fashioned* way of life.
a. modern
(b.) opposite of "modern"
c. foolish
d. uneducated

1. The Amish people live as people did in *former* times.
   a. farming
   b. land
   c. past
   d. contemporary

2. We make bread from dough, and we make dough from *flour*.
   a. flowers
   b. cake
   c. stove or oven
   d. ground wheat

3. The Amish people never *assimilated* into modern American society.
   a. became part of
   b. did not become part of
   c. opposite of "old-fashioned"
   d. separated from

4. The Amish community is one of many *subcultures* in the United States.
   a. bad cultures
   b. old-fashioned cultures
   c. small groups within a larger culture
   d. large groups containing smaller cultures

5. The Amish women don't wear *contemporary* fashions.
   a. old-fashioned
   b. beautiful
   c. of the present time
   d. of the past time

6. The Amish people use animals, and not tractors, to work the farm *land*.
   a. fruits and vegetables
   b. earth
   c. go from the air to the ground
   d. go from the ground to the air

7. The Amish women don't use lipstick or other types of *make-up*.
   a. cosmetics
   b. inventions
   c. clothing
   d. red

8. There are also Amish communities in other *sections* of the United States, not just Pennsylvania.
   a. religions
   b. rebels
   c. parts
   d. cities

9. Christianity and Islam are examples of *religions*.
   a. beliefs about Christ
   b. beliefs about Mohammed
   c. beliefs about Christ and Mohammed
   d. beliefs about God

10. Often, the Pennsylvania Dutch dialect today is a *mixture* of English vocabulary and German grammatical structure.
    a. separation
    b. mature
    c. combination
    d. language

Structure Practice

Write the appropriate verbs in the spaces provided. Use the present perfect progressive tense. Do not use the same verb more than one time.

build   **cook**   drive   live   wear   work

Example
a. The Amish women ___*have been cooking*___ their food on wood-burning stoves for the last few centuries.

1. The Amish people _____ horse-drawn wagons for almost three hundred years.

2. Amish farmers _____ their land with horses for the last few centuries.

3. The Amish people _____ their homes
   and furniture by hand since their settlement began.

4. The typical Amish woman _____ the
   same style clothing for almost three hundred years.

5. The Amish community _____ without
   electricity during the twentieth century.

Now write the negative forms of the verbs in the spaces provided. Use the present perfect progressive tense again. Do not use the same verb more than one time.

Example

    b. Most American people *haven't been cooking*

        their food on wood-burning stoves for the last few centuries.

6. Most American people _____ horse-
   drawn wagons for almost three hundred years.

7. Most American farmers _____ their
   land with horses for the last few centuries.

8. Most American people _____ their
   homes and furniture by hand for many years.

9. The typical American woman _____
   the same style clothing for almost three hundred years.

10. Most American communities _____
    without electricity during the twentieth century.

Group Activities

SMALL GROUP RETELLING AND DISCUSSION

Work with a small group of students. Each student in the group can retell some of the information in the reading "The Amish People and the Pennsylvania Dutch Country" until all the information has been retold. After that, each student can give his or her response to the way of life of the Amish people. Also, discuss the following questions with the members of your group: Do you think the Amish people will continue to live as they do, or will they eventually become part of the larger culture? What do you think of the way of life of the Amish? Do you think they should continue their way of life? Do you think their way of life is admirable in some way?

Also discuss: Are there groups in your country that live in a different way from most of the other people in the society? Have they been living in your country for a long time? What do most people in your country think of these people?

ROLE-PLAY

A couple of tourists ask some Amish people about their way of life. They ask the Amish to describe their way of life, and also to explain why they live as they do. What is the conversation? Write a dialogue to role-play for the rest of the class.

SIMON SAYS

Listen as your teacher tells you to act out the various emotions in this chapter and previous chapters. Act out the emotions and actions only if your teacher first says the words *Simon says*. If you make a mistake, you must sit down and stop playing the game. The last person left standing is the winner.

Possible commands are:

Sew.
Put a pie in the oven.
Drive a horse and wagon.
Hang up a sign.

Drive an automobile.
Cook some soup.
Taste some delicious pie.

MORE STRUCTURE PRACTICE: DISCUSSING TRADITIONS

Write the appropriate verbs in the spaces provided. Do not use the same verb more than one time.

drink   **eat**   give   kiss   put   wear

Example

Americans _____*have been eating*_____ turkey on Thanksgiving for many generations.

1. Americans _____ champagne on New Year's Eve for many, many years.

2. Americans _____ at midnight on New Year's Eve for many, many years.

3. Americans _____ costumes on Halloween for a long, long time.

4. Americans _____ presents to families and friends on their birthdays for centuries.

5. Americans _____ candles on birthday cakes for many, many years.

Now discuss some traditions in your country. What are some customs people in your country have been practicing for many years?

Example

People in Japan have been eating rice cakes on the New Year for many generations.

_____

_____

_____

_____

A RECIPE FOR SHOOFLY PIE

Perhaps you or one of your classmates would like to try making this traditional Pennsylvania Dutch dessert:

¾ cup flour
1 teaspoon sugar
½ cup brown sugar
⅛ cup butter

¼ cup molasses
¼ cup hot water
¼ teaspoon baking soda

Mix the flour and sugar together in a bowl. Add the butter and mix well.

In *another* bowl, mix the molasses, water, and baking soda.

Put the mixture into a *pastry shell* (see page 194). Bake at 400°F for 30 minutes.

Pastry Shell Recipe

You can buy a pastry shell or make one. If you would like to make one, here is a recipe:

1½ cups flour	½ cup cooking oil
½ teaspoon salt	3 tablespoons cold water

Mix the flour and salt together. Add the oil and mix well. Add the water, little by little. Mix with a fork after you add the water. Roll the mixture on a floured board. Then, put it into a pie pan. The mixture should cover the bottom and sides of the pie pan.

Williamsburg, Virginia: A Historic Colonial City

If you want to know more about the way of life of America's early settlers, one place to visit is Williamsburg, Virginia. Williamsburg is an old colonial[a] city that has been standing since the eighteenth century. The buildings in this city are in their original form—they look the same as they did over two hundred years ago when the Williamsburg community first began.

In the 1920s, the U.S. government decided to make Williamsburg a national landmark,[b] and architects[c] worked to preserve[d] and restore[e] the original colonial buildings. So, today, we can see the homes and businesses of the early settlers. Guides,[f] dressed in eighteenth-century clothing, take visitors on tours of the city. Some give demonstrations of colonial craft-making, such as candle-making, jewelry-making,[g] silversmithing,[h] and gunsmithing.[i]

Visitors can also eat colonial-style food in the old-time restaurants or taverns[j] of the city. Many famous Americans of the past ate in the taverns and walked through the streets of Williamsburg. These included George Washington and Thomas Jefferson, the first and third presidents of the United States, and Patrick Henry, the famous colonial statesman.

People from all over the world visit colonial Williamsburg, a living museum of early American life.

[a]relating to the original 13 colonies that formed the United States before the American Revolution   [b]a place of special historic interest   [c]people who design buildings and supervise their construction   [d] to save; to keep safe from injury or destruction   [e]renew; put something into its original state   [f]people who give information and explain points of interest   [g]making of items such as bracelets, rings, necklaces, etc.   [h]making of silverware   [i]designing, making, and repairing of guns   [j]bars; places where alcoholic drinks and generally some food are served

Skim the above reading, and write the main idea in one or two sentences:

_____

_____

Now scan the reading for the following information:

1. How old is the colonial city of Williamsburg?

   _____

2. What kinds of buildings can we see in Williamsburg?

   _____

3. What happened in the 1920s?

   _____

4. What can visitors see today in Williamsburg?

   _____

5. What kind of clothing do the guides in Williamsburg wear?

   _____

6. What kinds of demonstrations can visitors see in Williamsburg?

   _____

7. What kind of food is served in the taverns of the city?

   _____

8. What famous Americans of the past were familiar figures in Williamsburg?

   _____

chapter 14

Let's Celebrate! It's Halloween!

Review of Present Perfect Progressive, Unreal Conditional; Introduction of Verb + Gerund

Pre-reading Questions

Do you know the holiday called *Halloween?*

Do people celebrate this holiday everywhere in the world?

What do people do on this holiday?

What is your favorite holiday in your native country?

Did you ever miss this holiday because you were staying in another country?

Look at the pictures and tell what you see.

Let's Celebrate! It's Halloween!

Lately, I've been wishing I were back home. Today is October thirty-first. It's Halloween in the United States! Halloween is my favorite holiday of the year. But, here I am, three thousand miles away from New York City—my city.

My name is Mark, and I'm an art student in Italy. I've been living and studying in Italy for almost a year. I usually enjoy being in Italy, but today I've been feeling very homesick. I'm missing all the fun back home in the States.[1]

On Halloween, people really have a good time. Children dress up in all different kinds of costumes. They go to neighbors' houses and say, "Trick or treat." The neighbors give them a "treat"—usually candy, apples, or pennies. A lot of adults enjoy wearing costumes, too. They often put them on for parties.[2]

In New York City, where I come from, there is a Halloween parade. This parade has been taking place every year since 1970 in New York City's Greenwich Village, an area where, traditionally, many artists have lived and worked. People dress up in all sorts of wonderful, creative, funny costumes and join the parade. Sometimes, two or three people wear one costume together. One year, I saw several people dressed up as one huge, pink elephant! Many people spend a lot of time planning and making their costumes. I miss seeing all the people marching through the Greenwich Village streets and along Fifth Avenue in their costumes.[3]

Traditionally, the most popular disguises on Halloween are witches, ghosts, and skeletons. This is because a long, long time ago, people believed that the spirits of the dead walked the earth on October thirty-first. Halloween was originally a religious holiday that began in Ireland and Scotland in the year 1000 B.C. First, it was a Celtic holy day, and later, a Christian one.[4]

Nowadays, in the United States, Halloween no longer has a religious meaning for most people. Americans have been celebrating Halloween for over one hundred years, ever since the Irish and Scottish settlers brought their traditions with them. The majority of Americans don't know much about the history of the holiday. For most people, Halloween is just a day to have a lot of fun and go a little bit crazy.[5]

If I were back home in New York now, I'd put on a wild costume and go to the Halloween parade. But the fact is that I'm here in Florence, Italy. So, I won't put on a costume, but I will do a painting of Halloween in New York. In this way, I can share my favorite holiday with my Italian friends.[6]

1. Who is Mark?
   Where is he from?
   Where is he now?
   What has he been wishing lately?
   Why has he been feeling homesick?

Does he usually enjoy being in Italy?
How long has he been living and studying in Italy?
2. Do people usually enjoy Halloween?
What do children do on Halloween?
What do their neighbors do?
What do adults enjoy doing on Halloween?
3. What happens in New York City on Halloween?
How long has this parade been taking place?
Where in New York City has this parade been taking place?
What kind of people often live and work in Greenwich Village?
What do people do in the parade?
What did Mark see one year?
What does Mark miss seeing?
4. Traditionally, what are the most popular costumes on Halloween?
Why are these types of costumes popular?
What kind of holiday was Halloween originally?
In what countries did Halloween begin? What year?
5. Is Halloween a religious holiday in the United States?
How long have Americans been celebrating Halloween?
Do most Americans know a lot about the history of Halloween?
What kind of day is Halloween for most Americans?
6. What would Mark do if he were in New York?
Is Mark going to wear a costume in Italy to celebrate Halloween?
What is Mark going to do?

Introduction of Verb + Gerund

Some verbs in English must be followed by a *gerund* (verb + ing) instead of *to + base form:*

subject	verb	gerund verb + -ing	object/complement
He	enjoys	wearing	costumes.
He	misses	watching	the parade

Below are some more common verbs and expressions that must be followed by a gerund:

avoid	have problems	suggest
be interested in	keep on	think about
finish	spend time	

PRACTICE WITH VERB + GERUND

Write the gerund form of the verbs in parentheses in the spaces provided:

Example

On Halloween, many people enjoy _**going**_ to parties.
(go)

1. On Halloween, many people enjoy _____ costumes.
(wear)

2. Some people spend a lot of time _____ their Halloween costumes.
(make)

3. Mark misses _____ all the people on the streets in their Halloween costumes.
(see)

4. Mark enjoys _____ in the Halloween parade.
(march)

5. Mark misses _____ in New York on Halloween.
(be)

Vocabulary

Write the appropriate verbs in the spaces provided. Do not use the same verb more than one time. Be sure to use the correct tense of the verb that is needed.

celebrate	have fun	miss
dress up	join	put on
give a party	march	**wear**

Example

a. People _**wear**_ different kinds of costumes on Halloween.

1. Americans always _____ Halloween on October thirty-first.

2. In many countries, people _____ in parades on holidays.

3. On Halloween, people take off their usual clothes and _____ interesting costumes.

4. Some people like to _____ on Halloween. Their guests usually _____ in costumes.

5. In New York City, any person can put on a costume and _____ in the Halloween parade.

6. Both children and adults _____ on Halloween. It's a happy day for everyone.

Now supply the appropriate noun. Do not use the same word more than one time.

area	elephant	mile	skeleton
artist	ghost	neighbor	sort
candy	history	painting	spirit
costume	**holiday**	parade	treat
dead	majority	party	trick
earth	meaning	settler	

Example

b. Halloween is Mark's favorite *holiday* .

7. The _____ of people in the United States don't know much about the _____ of Halloween.

8. The Irish and Scottish _____ brought the Halloween tradition with them to the United States.

9. In many countries around the world, people march in _____ on holidays.

10. Often, people like to give a _____ on Halloween. They ask the guests to wear _____.

11. People wear all different _____ of costumes on Halloween.

12. _____ is one kind of _____ that children receive on Halloween.

13. Greenwich Village is an _____ of New York City where many _____ live and work.

14. Our planet is called the _____.

15. In museums, we can find _____ by many famous artists.

16. An _____ is a very large gray animal with a very long nose called a trunk.

17. That animal is not moving or breathing. I think it is _____.

18. Our skin and blood cover our bones, or the _____ of our bodies.

19. What is the _____ of this word?

20. The distance from New York to California is about three thousand _____.

21. The children played a _____ on their father. They gave him salt for his coffee instead of sugar!

22. Every person has a physical body which others can see and touch, and a non-physical _____ which no one can see or touch.

23. A long time ago, people believed that _____, or spirits of the dead, walked the earth on Halloween.

24. _____ are people who live near each other in the same community.

Now supply the appropriate adjective.

art	creative	**homesick**	wild
Celtic	holy	huge	wonderful

> **Example**
> c. On Halloween, Mark missed New York. He felt very
> *homesick* for his native city.

25. The _____ people lived in Ireland and Scotland before Christian times.

26. Originally, Halloween had a religious meaning. It was a _____ day for the Celtic people and, later on, for the Christians.

27. An elephant is not a small animal. It's really a _____ one.

28. We really enjoyed going to the Halloween party. We had a _____ time!

29. Artists are very imaginative and _____ people. They are always thinking of new and original things.

30. There are many famous _____ museums in New York City with beautiful paintings by great artists.

31. People don't have to wear their usual, normal clothes on Halloween. They can let their imaginations be free, and wear _____ costumes if they like.

Now supply the appropriate preposition. You can use the same word more than one time.

about	for	in	**on**
at	from	of	to

Example
d. Halloween is __*on*__ October thirty-first.

32. Halloween is _____ October.

33. Americans have been celebrating Halloween _____ over one hundred years.

34. A lot _____ people wear costumes _____ Halloween.

35. If Mark were _____ New York, he would dress up _____ a wild costume.

36. It's difficult to say exactly when Halloween began, but it was probably _____ 1000 B.C.

37. Mark enjoys going _____ the Halloween parade.

38. Mark comes _____ New York City. Now he is studying _____ the university in Florence, Italy.

39. _____ Halloween, Mark likes to take off his usual clothes, dress up _____ a costume, and march _____ the Halloween parade.

Dictation/Cloze

Listen as your teacher reads, and write the words that you hear in the blank spaces.

Mark is _____ _____ American. He _____
              1   2   3

_____ _____ at _____ university _____
    4   5   6   7

Florence, Italy _____ almost a year. He generally _____
                     8   9

_____ in Italy, but _____ Halloween he _____
   10   11   12

_____ in New York, his native city. Mark _____ a lot
   13   14

_____ fun _____ New York _____ Halloween.
   15   16   17

He _____ _____ _____ a costume and _____
      18   19   20   21

in the Halloween parade _____ Greenwich _____. He
                         22   23

_____ _____ all the people _____ the streets
   24   25   26

_____ their _____ and _____ Halloween cos-
   27   28   29

tumes. Some people spend all year _____ and _____
                                  30   31

their parade costumes.

Mark also _____ _____ to Halloween parties and
                  32   33

_____ the party food. He _____ _____ spicy,
   34   35   36

hot apple cider, and _____ delicious pumpkin pie.
                          37

Pumpkins are a very popular fruit on Halloween. In addition to

_____ them in pies, many people also _____ _____
   38   39   40

frightening or funny faces in them. These pumpkins with faces are called

"jack-o-lanterns." Mark _____ _____ all the jack-o-lanterns
                                      41   42

in the windows _____ houses and shops on Halloween.
                              43

    If Mark _____ in New York now, he _____
                           44   45

_____ _____ through the streets and _____ a
     46   47   48

lot _____ fun _____ Greenwich Village. But, _____
        49   50   51

in Italy. So, instead, _____ do a _____ of a New York
                              52   53

Halloween scene. _____ this way, he can _____ his
                           54   55

_____ holiday _____ his friends _____
     56   57   58

Florence.

Reading Comprehension

Circle the letter of the correct answers to the following questions:

1. The main idea of this reading passage is:
   a. An American student's adventures in Italy.
   b. A description of many different types of Halloween costumes.
   c. A homesick American describes his favorite holiday, Halloween.
   d. The history of Halloween.

2. A detail of this reading passage is:
   a. Americans wear wild costumes every day of the year.
   b. People in the United States began celebrating Halloween thousands of years ago.
   c. People like to eat jack-o-lanterns on Halloween.
   d. People like to dress up in different kinds of costumes on Halloween.

3. Which of the following sentences is true according to the reading passage?
   a. Only children celebrate Halloween in the United States.
   b. Children give candy and apples to adults on Halloween.
   c. Americans brought Halloween traditions to Ireland and Scotland.
   d. A long time ago, Halloween was a religious holiday.

4. Which of the following sentences is *not* true according to the reading passage?

    a. A long time ago, people believed that ghosts walked the earth on October thirty-first.

    b. For most Americans, Halloween is still a religious holiday.

    c. Mark is an art student at the university in Florence.

    d. Halloween was originally a Celtic holy day.

5. In your opinion, based on the reading passage, which of the following sentences is true?

    a. For Mark, Halloween has a religious meaning.

    b. Only Americans of Irish and Scottish origins celebrate Halloween.

    c. Americans don't like to live in other countries.

    d. People in Italy don't celebrate Halloween.

6. Which pair has the words that are most similar in meaning?

    a. *trick* and *treat*

    b. *holy* and *religious*

    c. *party* and *parade*

    d. *holiday* and *custom*

Guessing Meanings from Context

Guess the meaning of the italicized words from the context. Circle the letter of the word or words that are most similar in meaning to the italicized word(s):

Example

One Halloween, Mark saw several people dressed up as one *enormous* pink elephant!

    ⓐ huge

    b. color

    c. animal

    d. costume

1. Children are not the only ones who wear costumes on Halloween. There are also *quite a few* adults who wear them.

    a. quiet

    b. not many

    c. a lot of

    d. very few

2. A long, long time ago, people believed that the *souls* of the dead walked the earth on Halloween.
   a. skeletons
   b. spirits
   c. bodies
   d. witches

3. The majority of Americans don't know much about the history of Halloween, but there is probably a *minority* of people in the United States who know a lot about the holiday's past.
   a. most people
   b. a smaller number
   c. very intelligent
   d. a larger number

4. Halloween *originated* in Ireland and Scotland.
   a. first began
   b. ended
   c. no longer exists
   d. Britain

5. Lots of people dress up in *wild* costumes for the Halloween parade.
   a. big
   b. usual clothes
   c. witch
   d. very unusual and unconventional

6. *Wild* animals must live in forests and jungles. They cannot live in people's homes as pets.
   a. unusual
   b. big
   c. gentle and tame
   d. untamed, in a state of nature

7. People in the United States have been celebrating Halloween for *over* a century.
   a. more than
   b. less than
   c. almost
   d. finished

8. Mark wanted to *share* his favorite holiday with his friends in Italy by painting a Halloween scene.
   a. talk about
   b. show

   c. experience with others
   d. experience alone

9. My friend and I *share* an apartment together.
   a. show
   b. single
   c. use in common; divide
   d. clean and cook

10. Mark felt *nostalgic* for New York City on Halloween.
   a. nothing
   b. homesick
   c. bored
   d. holiday time

Practice with Ordinal Numbers

In English, we generally use *ordinal* numbers for dates and names of streets, avenues, roads, boulevards, etc. Below is a list of ordinal numbers:

first (1st)	eleventh (11th)	twenty-first (21st)
second (2nd)	twelfth (12th)	thirtieth (30th)
third (3rd)	thirteenth (13th)	**thirty-first (31st)**
fourth (4th)	fourteenth (14th)	*etc.*
fifth (5th)	fifteenth (15th)	fortieth (40th)
sixth (6th)	sixteenth (16th)	fiftieth (50th)
seventh (7th)	seventeenth (17th)	sixtieth (60th)
eighth (8th)	eighteenth (18th)	seventieth (70th)
ninth (9th)	nineteenth (19th)	eightieth (80th)
tenth (10th)	twentieth (20th)	ninetieth (90th)
		hundredth (100th)

Write the word forms of the ordinal numbers in parentheses in the spaces provided:

Examples
a. Halloween is on October *thirty-first*.
                            (31st)

b. The Halloween parade in New York marches on *Fifth*
                                    (5th)
   Avenue.

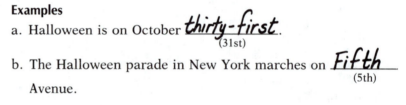

1. Thanksgiving is always on the _____ Thursday in November.
                                         (4th)

2. In 1984, Thanksgiving was on November _____.

(22nd)

3. In New York City, the famous Thanksgiving Day Parade marches through the streets of Manhattan and ends at _____ St.

(34th)

4. Americans celebrate Independence Day on the _____ of July.

(4th)

5. In the year 1976, Americans celebrated the _____ birthday of the United States of America.

(200th)

Using ordinal numbers, tell about some important dates in your country.

_____

_____

_____

_____

_____

Group Activities

SMALL GROUP RETELLING AND DISCUSSION

Work with a small group of students. Each student in the group can retell some of the information in the reading "Let's Celebrate! It's Halloween!" until all the information has been retold.

After that, each student in the group can describe a favorite holiday in his or her country. What do people do on this day? What kind of clothes do they wear? What kind of food do they enjoy eating on this day? Do people spend a lot of time preparing meals on this day? Do they give and receive gifts? Do they go to parties and dance? Why do they celebrate this holiday? Do you miss being away from home on this holiday? One student can write down the information that each person in the group gives, and later report it to the rest of the class.

MAKING A JACK-O-LANTERN
(TOTAL PHYSICAL RESPONSE/LISTENING EXERCISE)

We know that Americans often make jack-o-lanterns for Halloween by cutting funny or frightening faces in pumpkins. Sometimes, however, they make jack-o-lanterns by *drawing* a face on the pumpkin. If your class can get a pumpkin and some special drawing crayons, you can all make a jack-o-lantern together. Here's how:

The teacher or one student can go to the front of the class with the pumpkin and the crayons. The rest of the class can direct the teacher or student in drawing a face on the pumpkin. Each of the students can give a drawing instruction. For example:

First student: "Pick up the black crayon."

Second student: "Draw two large eyes on the pumpkin."

Third student: "Pick up the red crayon."

Fourth student: "Draw a big, smiling mouth on the pumpkin."

Go on like this until each student has given an instruction and the jack-o-lantern face is finished.

The person in the front of the class will follow the instructions only if the student gives them in *correct* English.

MAKING HALLOWEEN COSTUMES
(TOTAL PHYSICAL RESPONSE/LISTENING EXERCISE)

Perhaps for just one day, students can bring various items to class—pieces of material, scarves, maybe a few inexpensive bracelets and necklaces, and some make-up. These items can be displayed in front of the class so that all the students can see them.

Two students, student A and student B, can go to the front of the class. Student A will make a Halloween costume for student B. The other students in the class will direct student A in making the costume. Each of the students can give one instruction for creating the costume. For example:

First student: "Pick up the blue scarf."

Second student: "Put it on student B's head."

Third student: "Pick up the black make-up."

Fourth student: "Draw a mustache on student B."

The students can continue giving instructions until the costume is completed. Then another pair of students can go to the front of the class, another costume can be made, and so on, until everyone has a costume.

Student A will follow the instructions of the other students only if they are given in *correct* English.

After, the students can vote for the best costume in a "Costume Contest."

A HALLOWEEN TRICK AND A TREAT

Perhaps at some time you or your classmates will have the chance to play this traditional Halloween game. The game is called *Dunking for Apples*. It is sometimes played at Halloween parties.

Put about eight or ten apples in a large pan of water. Put a coin inside one of the apples. Players approach the pan one at a time. They put their hands behind their backs and try to pick up an apple using only their teeth. The person who picks up the apple with the coin inside will have a lucky year, and also win a prize.

Read the instructions above for the game several times. Then, without looking at the page, tell the rest of the class how the game is played.

A HALLOWEEN TREAT: A RECIPE FOR PUMPKIN PIE

Perhaps at some time, you or your classmates will have the chance to try this traditional Halloween dessert:

2 cups cooked pumpkin (see following recipe)	1/2 teaspoon cinnamon
	1/2 teaspoon nutmeg
4 eggs, separated	1/3 cup milk
1 cup sugar	1/3 cup oil
1 tablespoon corn starch	

First, break the eggs and separate the yellow part (the *yolk*) from the white part (the *egg white*). Beat the yolks a little bit. Mix together the egg yolks, cooked pumpkin, sugar, corn starch, and cinnamon. Then add the milk, oil, and nutmeg.

In another bowl, beat the egg whites until they are stiff, and add them

to the pumpkin mixture. Mix everything together *slowly*. Pour the mixture into a 9-inch pastry shell (see recipe in Chapter 13) and bake the pie at 375°F for 45 minutes.

RECIPE FOR COOKED PUMPKIN

You can buy cooked pumpkin in a can in the supermarket, or you can make it yourself. If you prefer to make it, here is a recipe:

First, wash a large pumpkin and cut it in half. Put the two halves face

down in a pan. Put it into the oven and cook it at 375°F until it is soft. Then, take out the soft inside of the pumpkin with a spoon or a fork. Put it into a colander and drain it overnight. The next morning, put the pumpkin into a bowl and mix it until it is very smooth. Then, drain it again.

Greenwich Village

Greenwich Village is a place in New York City where many artists have been living and working since the nineteenth century. At that time, a small group of artists and writers began to meet in the cafés and bars of "the Village" to discuss[a] the newest and most modern ideas in art and literature. By the early 1900s, Greenwich Village was well known as a place where artists with different or unconventional[b] views[c] about art, and other people with generally unusual or non-conformist[d] life-styles,[e] spent their time.

The bohemian[f] life of Paris had a great influence[g] on the gradual creation of Greenwich Village as New York's bohemian, "avant-garde"[h] center. There is even an imitation of Paris' famous Arch of Triumph in the center of Greenwich Village, Washington Square Park.

In 1917, the famous French avant-garde artist, Marcel Duchamp, a resident[i] of the Village, climbed to the top of the Washington Square arch and declared Greenwich Village a separate, independent "nation of bohemians." Such outrageous[j] and eccentric behavior became more and more typical of Greenwich Villagers, and began to attract tourists from everywhere.

In the 1920s, there was also something else in Greenwich Village which attracted tourists—alcohol! The 1920s was the Era of Prohibition in the United States; the buying and selling of alcoholic drinks was illegal.[k] But, in Greenwich Village, there were many secret bars called "speakeasies" where people could buy alcohol. Today, there is a famous bar in Greenwich Village called *Chumley's,* which was once a speakeasy. A lot of famous artists and writers went to this bar— among them, the playwright Eugene O'Neill and the poet Edna St. Vincent Millay.

Chumley's is still popular with Greenwich Villagers, and also with the many tourists who walk along the Greenwich Village streets in search[l] of art galleries, cafés, and that special "bohemian spirit."

---

[a]talk about [b]not usual or ordinary; original [c]opinions [d]different from what is usual [e]ways of living [f]persons (usually artists or writers) who have unusual, unconventional life-styles [g]effect [h]new and experimental ideas in art [i]a person who lives in a place; inhabitant [j]very, very unconventional [k]not legal; against the law [l]looking for

Skim the reading on page 213 and write the main idea in one or two sentences:

_____

_____

Now scan the reading for the following information:

1. When did artists and writers first begin to meet in Greenwich Village?

_____

2. What kinds of things did they talk about?

_____

3. What was Greenwich Village well known for by the early twentieth century?

_____

4. What other city influenced the development of Greenwich Village?

_____

5. What can you find in Washington Square Park?

_____

6. Who was Marcel Duchamp? What did he do in 1917?

_____

7. What two things began to attract more and more tourists to Greenwich Village?

_____

8. What was Prohibition?

_____

9. What were speakeasies?

_____

10. What is *Chumley's?*

_____

11. Name two famous writers who went to Chumley's in the 1920s.

_____

12. Who goes to *Chumley's* today?

_____

13. Why do tourists come to Greenwich Village today?

_____

4 Bottles of wine   14 records 10-15 tapes   5 packages of nuts
12 Dishes   2 cakes (Maria, Fernando)

chapter 15

Planning a Class Party

Countables and Uncountables

Pre-reading Questions

Look at the pictures and tell what you see.

Is it usual for students to have a class party at the end of the semester in your country?

What kinds of food do students prepare and bring to the party? Is there alcohol at the party? Are there soft drinks?

Planning a Class Party

It's hard to believe that the last day of class is fast approaching. The students in our class have been working and studying all semester. Now it's time to relax and have some fun! Let's have a party! Perhaps all the students can get together and decide what we will need for our celebration. Let's see:

How many students will come to the party?

How much food will we need at the party? How many international dishes? How many people can bring dishes from their native countries?

Should we have wine at the party? How much wine? How many bottles?

How much music can the students supply? How many tapes and records?

How much cake will we need? How many pieces of cake will each person probably eat?

How much snack food will we need? How many packages of nuts, potato chips, and others?

How much fruit should we get? How many apples, bananas, pears, melons, bunches of grapes, etc?

How much soda will everyone drink? How many different kinds of soft drinks?

How many cups, plates, and napkins will be necessary?

How much silverware will we need? How many forks, knives, and spoons?

Perhaps one or two students can go to the front of the class and ask the rest of the students these questions. Then, they can write on the board how much or how many of each item each of the students can bring.

Countables and Uncountables

In English, we have two kinds of nouns. Some nouns are in a form that we can count. These are *countables* (or *count nouns*). Some nouns, however, are *uncountables* (or *non-count nouns*). For example, it's not really possible to count water or wine. However, we can count *glasses of water* or *bottles of wine*. It's not really possible to count food. However, we can count *dishes* or *plates of food*. The glasses, bottles, and dishes give these nouns a form that we can count. We use *much* with uncountable nouns and *many* with countable nouns:

	much	**uncountable noun**	
How	much	water	is on the table?
How	much	food	is on the table?

	many	**countable noun**	
How	many	glasses of water	are on the table?
How	many	dishes of food	are on the table?

In general, nouns that have plurals are in a countable form. Nouns that don't have plurals are not.

PRACTICE WITH *MUCH* AND *MANY*

Decide if the nouns in the sentences below are countable or uncountable. Write either *much* or *many* in the blank spaces:

> **Example**
> a. How _**much**_ cake do we need?
> b. How _**many**_ pieces of cake do we need?

1. How _____ milk did you buy?

2. How _____ bottles of milk did you buy?

3. How _____ plates of ice cream did he eat?

4. How _____ ice cream did he eat?

5. How _____ cheese is on the plate?

6. How _____ pieces of cheese are on the plate?

7. How _____ slices of bread are left?

8. How _____ bread is left?

9. How _____ time do we have for our party?

10. How _____ hours do we have for our party?

Vocabulary: New and Review

Write the appropriate verbs in the spaces provided. Do not use the same verb more than one time.

approach	have fun	**relax**
get together	plan	supply
have a party		

Example

a. After working all day, we finally had the chance to sit down and _**relax**_____.

1. Let's celebrate the end of the semester. Let's _____ on the last day of class.

2. All the students can _____ and decide what we will need for the party.

3. I think all the students will really enjoy themselves and _____ at the party.

4. Do you _____ to come to the party?

5. The last day of class is almost here. It's _____ very fast.

6. The students will _____ the food, drink, and music for the party.

Now supply the appropriate noun:

bottle	knife	record	soda
celebration	nuts	silverware	soft drink
cups	piece	snack	tape
fork	potato chip		

Example

b. How many _**bottles**_____ of wine will we need for the party?

7. How many _____ of cake will each person eat?

8. Every party has to have music! We can play _____ on our record player and _____ on our tape recorder.

9. Hard liquor contains alcohol, but a _____ doesn't.

10. _____ is a drink that contains carbonated gas.

11. If we cut potatoes into very thin slices, then fry them and salt them, we have _____.

12. When people are hungry between meals, they often eat a

    _____ .

13. Generally, we pour wine into glasses and coffee into _____ .

14. We cut our food with a _____ .

15. We eat our food with a _____ .

16. _____ includes forks, knives, and spoons.

17. _____ are a nutritious snack. People like them, and so do

    squirrels.

18. A party is one type of _____ .

Supply the appropriate noun, using these nouns for names of fruits.

    apple   banana   grapes   melon   pear

19. An _____ is usually round and red.

20. _____ are small, round purple or green fruits. We use them

    to make wine.

21. A _____ is a long yellow fruit.

22. A _____ is a large round fruit that is usually orange or green

    on the inside. We often eat it for dessert.

23. A _____ is a fruit that is fat at the bottom but thinner at the

    top.

Now supply the appropriate preposition. You may use the same word
more than one time.

    for   in   of   on   **to**

> **Example**
> c. How many students will come __*to*__ the party?

24. There will be many different kinds _____ dishes at the party.

25. Maybe one or two students can come _____ the front _____ the

    class and write _____ the board what each student can bring.

26. Most _____ the students _____ the class want to bring food from their native countries.

27. We will also need wine and soft drinks _____ the party.

28. Students who don't have time to cook can bring packages _____ snack foods _____ the party.

Dictation/Cloze

Listen as your teacher reads, and write the words that you hear in the blank spaces.

The students in _____ class _____ _____
                         1   2   3

_____ and _____ hard _____ semester. Now
   4   5   6

_____ time to _____ and _____ some
   7   8   9

_____. Why _____ we _____ a party? Let's
   10   11   12

_____ _____ and _____ what we _____
  13   14   15   16

need for our _____.
       17

How _____ _____ will we need at the party? How
     18   19

_____ international _____? How _____
  20   21   22

_____ can bring dishes from _____ native _____?
  23   24   25

How _____ _____ can the students _____?
     26   27   28

How _____ records or how _____ _____ can
     29   30   31

each person _____?
       32

How _____ _____ of _____, potato chips,
     33   34   35

and other _____ foods _____ we need?
     36   37

How _____ _____ and _____ should we
          38   39   40

_____? How _____ _____ do we need?
  41   42   43

How _____ _____ will we _____ at the
        44   45   46

party? Everyone will _____ so _____ _____
                      47   48   49

that no one _____ _____ to leave!
         50   51

Reading Comprehension

Decide if the following sentences are true or false according to the reading passage. Write *T* for *true* or *F* for *false* on the line after each statement:

1. The last day of class is almost here. _____

2. The students have been very lazy all semester. _____

3. One student can decide what we will need for the celebration. _____

4. Perhaps some students can bring typical food of their native countries. _____

5. The students can watch television at the party. _____

6. Perhaps some students can bring alcohol to the party. _____

7. There will probably be more than one type of soft drink at the party.

   _____

8. Probably no one will listen to music or dance at the party. _____

Guessing Meanings from Context

Guess the meanings of the italicized words from the context. Circle the letter of the word or words that are most similar in meaning to the italicized word(s):

Example

It's *hard* to believe that the last day of the class is fast approaching. The time has been going so quickly!
  a. easy
  b. difficult
  c. opposite of "soft"
  d. hurry

1. Almost everyone is in a *festive* mood at a party.
   a. depressed
   b. bad
   c. happy
   d. celebration

2. The last day of class is coming soon. The semester is *drawing to a close.*
   a. almost finished
   b. just beginning
   c. approaching
   d. picture

3. At parties, people often drink beer, wine, and other types of *liquor*.
   a. liquid
   b. whiskey
   c. soft drinks
   d. alcohol

4. Having fun at a party is a good way to release *tension*.
   a. enjoy
   b. friends
   c. stress, nervousness
   d. gifts, presents

5. For *entertainment* at parties, people like to dance, play games, talk, and eat.
   a. entering
   b. celebrate
   c. fun, amusement
   d. friendly, nice

6. The last day of class is almost here. Soon it will be the end of the *term*.
   a. party
   b. day
   c. year
   d. semester

PARTY IDIOMS

Guess the meanings of the italicized expressions below from the context. Discuss the possible meanings with the class:

1. Last year our class had a wonderful party. Everyone *had a ball!*
2. This year's party will be great, too. If you come, you will *have the time of your life!*

3. At a party, my friend Allan is always the center of attention because he's so charming and funny. Everyone says he's *the life of the party*.
4. Students often like to *throw a party* at the end of the semester.
5. On weekends, American college students sometimes have a beer *bash*.

Now answer the following questions using the above expressions in your sentences. Do not use the same expression more than once:

1. Will the teacher enjoy the class party this year?
   Yes. She will have the time of her life.

2. Which of the students in our class will be the center of attention this year?

   _____

3. Do all the students want to have a celebration at the end of the semester?

   _____

4. What kind of weekend celebration do American college students sometimes have?

   _____

5. Will the students have a good time at the party this year?

   _____

Group Activities

SMALL GROUP RETELLING AND DISCUSSION

Work with a small group of students. One student in the group can say the name of an item from the reading, such as *cake*. Another student in the group can form a question with that word, using *how much* or *how many*. For example, *How much cake do we need?* If the student makes a mistake, the other students in the group can help. Each student in the group will have a chance to say a party item and form a question.

After that, you can discuss the following questions with the members of your group: Is it usual for classes in your country to have parties? If so, what do the students do at these parties? Are the parties formal or informal? What kind of clothes do the students wear? What kind of food does everyone eat? Do students bring or prepare food for these parties? Does everyone listen to music and dance at these parties? Does everyone play party games? Do students drink alcohol at these parties?

Discuss other types of parties in your country. On what occasions is it usual for people to give parties? On birthdays? On anniversaries? After weddings? When a baby is born? When a student graduates from high school or college? Describe these parties. What do the guests do? What do they usually wear? What kind of food and drink is served? Do people bring gifts? Is there a special cake? Are there games? Do people send out invitations by mail before the party? Do they take photographs at the party?

In all countries, people enjoy going to parties for social reasons. However, in the United States, people sometimes go to parties for more practical reasons, also. At some parties, it's possible to meet "important people" and make "good business connections" or "career contacts." Is this true in your country too?

PARTY GAMES: TIC-TAC-TOE

Divide the class into two teams, the X team and the O team. Each team takes turns forming a correct question with *how much* or *how many* and one of the words on the tic-tac-toe board. At each turn, one member of each team chooses a word and forms a question. If there is no error in the question, the team gets either an X or an O in the word square. If there is an error in the question, the team does not get the X or O. The first team to receive a complete line of three X's or O's (horizontally, vertically, or diagonally) wins the game.

candy	bottle of soda	cheese
chair	box of crackers	fruit
snack	music	beer

Tic-tac-toe can be played to practice other vocabulary words and grammatical structures also.

GOSSIP: INVENT A STORY ABOUT ANOTHER STUDENT

Invent a story about a student in the class. You can write about all the things you think this student will do at the class party. For example:

> Nick will really dance a lot at the party. His feet will hurt for many days after. He'll eat too much food. He'll eat so many different kinds of dishes that he'll get a stomach ache. Nick will also drink a lot of wine. He'll drink so much wine that he'll be happy for hours.

If another student in the class disagrees with any part of this story, he or she can repeat it, making the sentences negative:

> Nick won't dance so much that his feet will hurt for days after the party. He won't eat too much food. . . . He won't drink a lot of wine. . . .

RECIPE FOR PARTY DIP

Try putting some of this delicious dip on your potato chips, pretzels, or crackers. The students can use the recipe to make the party dip in class:

1 cup mayonnaise	1/2 teaspoon paprika
3 tablespoons minced onion	1 clove garlic, minced
1 teaspoon salt	1 tablespoon mustard
1 cup sour cream	

Put all the above ingredients on a desk or table in front of the classroom. Also put a measuring cup, a bowl, and some measuring spoons there. Students can take turns coming to the front of the class in pairs. One student can direct the other in following the recipe. One student will give an instruction, and the other student will follow the instruction. For example:

Student A: Measure one cup of mayonnaise and put it into the bowl.
Student B will listen and follow the instruction.

Student C: Measure 3 tablespoons of minced onion and add it to the mayonnaise.
Student D will listen and follow the instruction.

Student E: Measure 1 tablespoon of mustard and add it to the mayonnaise and onion mixture. Then add 1 teaspoon of salt.

Student F will listen and follow the instruction.

Student G: Measure 1 cup of sour cream and add it to the mixture.
Student H will listen and follow the instruction.

Student I: Measure 1/2 teaspoon of paprika and add it to the mixture.
     Then put in the garlic. Mix everything together well.
Student J will listen and follow the instruction.

The rest of the class can make sure the students follow the instructions correctly. If a student makes a mistake, the rest of the class can help him or her by saying the instruction again, perhaps in different words.

When the students have finished making the recipe, everyone can enjoy dipping their snack foods into it and eating it!